Tea Party to Trump

A Political Revolution Unveiled

By
William Frye Sr.

Tea Party to Trump

A Political Revolution Unveiled

Contents

Introduction:
Stirring the Pot - The Inception of Revolutionary Ideas

The fabric of American politics is a patchwork, threads of diverse thought interwoven into a complex tapestry. At its most transformative junctures, this fabric ripples with the energy of revolutionary ideas, shaping the nation's course. This book embarks on an analytical journey tracing the shadowy lines from the insurgent Tea Party movement to the tumultuous Trump era, unveiling the connections that transcend mere chronology.

In the volatile world of politics, concepts like "revolutionary" take on a life all their own. They reside not in the material objects that can be touched or held, but in the sparks that fly from the friction of public discourse. The Tea Party movement proved to be such a catalyst, its inception rooted in the fertile ground of discontent and its growth powered by fervent convictions.

Revolutionary ideas don't emerge from a vacuum; they're born when the status quo fails to contain the swelling pressures of change. The Tea Party's meteoric rise was marked by a collective yearning for a return to perceived fiscal and constitutional purity. Their battle cry, a resonant echo of historical defiance, spoke to those who felt unheard by the monoliths of political power.

The movement's language, brimming with the rhetoric of rebellion and reform, captures the imagination and stirs the pot of the possible. It draws parallels not just with the ideological underpinnings of the American Revolution but also resonates with the broader human struggle for self-determination and representation.

While the Tea Party's tenets of limited government and fiscal responsibility took root in a conservative field, these seeds grew to influence the outcome of elections and the shape of policy alike. It didn't just alter the dynamic within the GOP; it cast long shadows that would influence its trajectory for years to come.

Ironically, the movement's vigor and vehemence laid the groundwork for what many view as an ideological successor—the phenomenon of Donald Trump's political ascendancy. Trump's rise to power carried the undertones of the Tea Party's revolutionary spirit, albeit in a form adorned with populism and the enigmatic allure of an outsider promising to upend the establishment.

The hallmark of Trump's campaign, and subsequent administration, was the capacity to channel the fervor of the Tea Party into a broader nationalistic and economic populism. Populism, in its essence, promises to return power to "the people," yet in practice it often consolidates power around a singular, polarizing figure.

However, the fusion of Tea Party ideology and Trump's unique brand of leadership doesn't imply a seamless transition—or that the Tea Party has maintained unblemished influence. Tensions within the conservative movement, and amongst GOP ranks, suggest a more complex relationship, fraught with ideological tugs-of-war and political maneuvering.

One's interpretation of this era, whether seen as utopian or dystopian, relies on the vantage point from which these waves of change are witnessed. The same movement that inspires hope in one part of the electorate can induce profound anxiety in another. The very underpinnings of the Tea Party and Trump era—a call to shake the foundations of government—can suggest both revival and rupture.

Through examining the Tea Party's influence on policy and governance, we begin to discern patterns in the subsequent Trump administration's approach. Legislative priorities, Supreme Court appointments, and a general push towards the conservative agenda are all elements that draw from, and in some cases, reinvent the movement's original playbook.

In the past, great movements have precipitated pivotal eras in American history, from the revolutionaries who forged a new nation to the civil rights leaders who reshaped our social fabric. The Tea Party's legacy—its direct link to the Trump era and its enduring impact on the Republican Party—promises to serve as yet another notable chapter in this unfolding historical narrative.

The true test of the Tea Party's revolutionary ideas may lie in their longevity and their ability to adapt and thrive in the evolving political landscape. Their resonance with the values and visions of subsequent conservative leaders and movements will either validate or vilify their place in the annals of American political history.

As we wade into a sea of retrospection and foresight, it is imperative to canvass not only the successes and failures of these political phenomena but also their lasting influence and potential legacy. For it is in the confluence of past and future that we can fully grasp the significance of these ideas that once shook the nation to its core.

This introduction serves as a portal into an exploration of these thoughts, ideologies, and events. By dissecting the strands that bind the Tea Party to the Trump era, we uncover not only the seeds of revolution in American politics but also the boundless potential for change—and the inevitable challenges such transitions entail.

Let us then proceed with a closer look at how a movement came, stirred the pot of the established order, and imprinted its revolutionary ideas onto the political landscape, setting the stage for a wave of change that would influence the highest echelons of power in the United

States. Welcome to the inception of revolutionary ideas that redefined an era.

Chapter 1:
The Genesis of the Tea Party Movement

The emergence of the Tea Party movement was a critical juncture in American political history, marked by a fiery amalgamation of grassroots activism, historical reverence, and a profound discontent with the status quo. It was in the nascent days of this movement that a new chapter in political efficacy began to pen itself, swiftly gaining momentum as a force to be reckoned with in the corridors of power. With the inauguration of President Barack Obama in 2009 and the subsequent economic interventions such as the bailout of banks, amidst rising skepticism over government's reach, conditions were ripe for a political renaissance of conservative ideals.

Manifesting first in hushed conversations, the ripples of dissent soon swelled into a tide that sought to inundate what many perceived as an overbearing government expansion. The core philosophy of the movement was relatively straightforward, yet potent: a call for a return to constitutional principles, limited government, and fiscal responsibility. Its rhetoric was charged with the fervor of revolution and the sanctity of American founding values.

Amidst a labyrinth of economic uncertainty, voices on talk radio, echo chambers on the internet, and commentary on cable news fostered a burgeoning identity for the Tea Party. Empowered by historical allusions to the Boston Tea Party, this contemporary movement fixated not on the harbouring of tea, but on what they saw as a modern-day taxation without representation.

While it may be tempting to pinpoint the exact moment the Tea Party emerged, it was, in fact, the culmination of multiple events and prevailing sentiments. It was not born from a single protest or charismatic leader, but rather forged by a shared constituency of concerns over government overreach and economic frustration. This ethos was harnessed and disseminated through slogans, imagery, and a resolute invocation of the Constitution as a guiding star in what was perceived as a twilight for American conservative values.

The ideological groundwork was in place for a seismic shift in the Republican Party and in the political landscape of the United States. Yet no one at that time could foresee how the undercurrents from this movement would flow unabated into the mainstream, eventually enveloping the party's strategy and setting the stage for the ascendancy of figures like Donald Trump. The Tea Party, once a fragmented amalgam of outraged voices, brokered unprecedented influence, paving the way for a brand of politics that would reshape the GOP and, indeed, the very fabric of partisan engagement in America.

But before the waves of change would crest, they first had to break from the surface, propelled by an unmistakable, fervid declaration that business as usual was no longer tenable. The genesis of the Tea Party Movement was as much about this declaration as it was about the specifics of its policy positions, seizing its moment in a world bracing for profound transformation.

The Blueprint: Origins and Key Influences

The birth of the Tea Party movement, like the inception of any transformative political wave, cannot be attributed to a single event, individual, or policy. Rather, it must be understood as a confluence of historical predispositions, contemporary grievances, and a burgeoning sense of disenfranchisement among a segment of Americans who felt alienated by the evolving national landscape.

Tracing its lineage, the Tea Party drew inspiration from the original Boston Tea Party of 1773—an act of protest against taxation without representation that festered into a revolution. This historical parallel was not just a symbolic adoption but also an ideological alignment with the espousal of limited government and the perceived right to resist overbearing authority. The rhetoric of freedom used by the Founding Fathers had found new life in the voices of modern conservatives who believed that their liberty was once again under threat.

This sentiment was stoked to a blaze by key influencers who, intentionally or not, laid the groundwork for the movement's ascendancy. Vocal conservative figures in media and politics fostered a climate ripe for a grassroots rebellion. It was a time marked by acute concern over the national debt, government bailouts, and the interventionist policies that followed the 2008 financial crisis. This period of tumult had engendered a collective angst that sought a target, and the tax policies of the new administration provided just that.

Enmeshed in these economic anxieties were broader fears—fears of cultural displacement and a sense that the 'real' America was fading into the shadows of globalism and multiculturalism. Threads of American exceptionalism were woven into the fabric of the movement, reinforcing a vision of returning to a perceived golden age of constitutional purity and national prowess. The stage was set for a political renaissance, a clarion call for a revolution of values that would challenge the status quo.

Each of these influences contributed to the architecture of the Tea Party phenomenon. They represented a tapestry of discontent that spread across demographics and geographies—an undercurrent of frustration waiting for a spark. The synthesis of these disparate forces, firmly rooted in fear of economic decline and socio-cultural erosion, gave birth to a grassroots movement that harnessed the power of collective identity and transformed the American political landscape in ways that continue to reverberate through the era of Donald Trump.

It's within this complex network of influences that the Tea Party mobilized, not simply as a reactionary force, but as a strategic reshaping of political activism. It sought not only to protest but to upend the system from within, paving the path for insurgencies that would follow and alter the face of conservative politics in the years to come. The Tea Party's rise was, in many ways, an overture to the symphony of change reverberating through America's right wing—a prelude to the populist fervor that would eventually sweep Donald Trump into the Oval Office.

Tax Day Protests: A Spark Ignites Turning the pages back to the early chapters of the Tea Party's story, the Tax Day protests of 2009 stand out as a pivotal moment. In the grassroots mythology, April 15 has long been symbolic—representing the citizen's duel with the tax collector, a date seared into the national psyche. Like lightning crackling through the charged atmosphere of American politics, these demonstrations lit the fuse of a new conservative era.

The Tax Day protests were more than just a collective outpouring of frustration. They were the crystallization of simmering resentments across a swath of the American electorate. Festering anxieties over government overreach, galloping spending, and the perceived erosion of constitutional liberties found their expression on the streets as thousands rallied, harking back to the defiance of the Boston Tea Party of 1773.

Those who assembled on April 15, 2009, shared a common narrative that taxes and government services had shifted beyond the bounds of reasonable civic duty. Tax codes had grown byzantine, while the government's balance sheet ballooned, evoking primeval fears of losing control—of their lives, their businesses, and their country's future.

Underneath the patriotic banners and DIY placards, the Tax Day protests unearthed a vein of populism that had lain dormant. These events weren't merely a disagreement with policy; they were an outright rebellion against the establishment. The protesters didn't exclusively target Democrats or Republicans; they directed their ire at any politician they held responsible for the perceived fiscal decline of the nation.

The language of these protests was potent, a unique blend of revolutionary fervor and constitutional veneration. The Tea Party moniker was both a clever acronym for "Taxed Enough Already" and a historical homage, cementing their actions within a storied tradition of American resistance. This was the kind of storytelling that blurs the lines between past and present, making every participant a character in the continuing saga of America's struggle for liberty.

The spark from the Tax Day protests kindled a fire that swept through American politics with surprising speed. Like many grassroots movements, the Tea Party's origins were diffuse, the result of multiple calls to action from various pundits and organizations. However, these protests served to unite disparate voices in a chorus that soon became impossible to ignore.

These demonstrations also attracted immense media attention—part curiosity, part bewilderment—with networks devoting extensive coverage to the events. Anchors and political commentators dissected the Tea Party's significance, while the images of the protests themselves helped to coalesce a network of activists who might otherwise never have known of each other's existence.

Interestingly, the spirit of the Tax Day protests can be traced forward into ensuing election cycles. The fervor from the street corner and town square found its way into the campaign strategies of Tea Party candidates. The rhetoric of fiscal restraint and limited government became not just planks in their platforms but core components of their political identities.

As these activists turned candidates infiltrated the political system, the Tea Party began reshaping the landscape of the Republican Party. The establishment, comfortable in their long-held seats of power, found themselves outflanked by insurgents who were more in tune with the Tax Day protestors' demands. The reverberations of April 15, 2009, were shaping elections and policies alike.

The Tax Day protests, in essence, were a casting call for new political champions. They emerged as true believers who had carried the banners, chanted slogans, and felt the thrill of solidarity that only collective action can inspire. Figures like Ted Cruz and Marco Rubio owe a debt to the Tax Day spark, as do many lesser-known figures in state and local governance.

The demonstrations were also a bellwether for the successes and limitations of the movement. While they energized a base and secured some electoral victories, the Tea Party also faced the inherent difficulties of maintaining grassroots passion within the structures of power. As they moved from protest to politics, the Tea Party was tested by the need to balance ideological purity with practical governance.

With the benefit of hindsight, the Tax Day protests can also be seen as a precursor to the populist wave that would eventually buoy Donald Trump to the presidency. The sentiments these protestors harbored—the distrust of elites, the disillusionment with conventional politics—laid the groundwork for Trump's 'Drain the Swamp' message.

The metamorphosis of tax protest into political ascendancy reveals much about the nature of contemporary American conservatism. The Tea Party had tapped into a deep well of civic unrest, a profound discomfort with the direction the country was heading. The Tax Day protests weren't an endpoint but rather the beginning of an ideological journey that would eventually find representation in the highest echelons of power.

Finally, while the Tax Day protests solidified the Tea Party movement, they also presented a cautionary tale for future movements. The transition from fiery protests to the more sedate halls of Congress implies a potential dilution of purpose. In galvanizing a political force, the Tea Party both capitalized on and contributed to the increasingly polarized state of American politics, setting the stage for the triumphs and tribulations to follow in subsequent chapters of this narrative.

The story of the Tax Day protests thus embodies a form of political theater where every act, every character, and every speech has resonated through time. It is a story where the echoes of the past continually whisper in the corridors of present power, a tale of a spark that ignited a movement and reshaped not just a party, but an entire political era.

Slogans, Symbols, and the Constitution

In the crucible of American politics, the Tea Party movement emerged not only with a platform of political ideals but also with an arsenal of slogans and symbols deeply rooted in the nation's historical consciousness. These elements served as banners proclaiming a new era while simultaneously summoning the ethos of the Revolutionary War era.

"Taxed Enough Already" became the battle cry of this nascent movement, weaving contemporary grievances of perceived overtaxation into the historical fabric of the nation's founding. It wasn't just a mantra; it encapsulated a principle that laid at the heart of early American defiance and, now, modern conservative dissent.

The Gadsden flag, with its fierce rattlesnake and stark warning "Don't Tread on Me", was resurrected with fervor. Its presence at Tea

Party rallies was both a symbol of resistance and a declaration of the movement's readiness to strike against what they saw as government overreach. Such imagery tapped into a deep-seated vein of American identity and the cherished value of liberty.

Equally, the stylized depictions of the Boston Tea Party became emblematic, heralding a call to arms against what participants deemed a rerun of historical injustice. This time, it wasn't a foreign monarchy overstepping but their own federal government, whose policies and actions clashed with the ideals of freedom and self-determination.

The rallying power of these symbols cannot be overstated; they galvanized a faction that saw themselves as heirs to the Constitution's originalist principles. The core belief that the government should be by the people, for the people, held fast, as did the conviction that federal authority should be curtailed in favor of states' rights and individual freedoms.

This movement didn't just appropriate the visual aspects of America's revolutionary spirit; they also embraced a strict, textual interpretation of the Constitution. Arguing that the nation had veered off course from its foundational legal document, Tea Party activists promoted a return to what they saw as Constitutional purity. The significance of this can't be understated – it provided an intellectual touchstone for their cause and a veneer of historical legitimacy.

Constitutional originalism became the philosophical cornerstone for many within the Tea Party. This adherence formed a link across time, presenting the Tea Party as stalwart defenders of an American creed supposedly being eroded by contemporary politics. They positioned themselves as not just reformers, but as restorers of a constitutional Eden.

Symbols and slogans became the currency of identity within the Tea Party, but they were only as potent as the beliefs and actions they inspired. Town halls and protests across the country bore witness to impassioned citizens, many draped in colonial garb, decrying the usurpation of their rights by Big Government.

These motifs and the constitutional fervor were not merely rhetorical devices; they resonated deeply with a large swathe of the American electorate. They painted an idyllic, albeit dystopian, vision of America's present juxtaposed against a utopian reference to its founding—creating a narrative that something precious had been lost and must be reclaimed.

This sentiment captured a particular demographic that felt alienated and voiceless within the larger political dialogue. They saw in the Tea Party a movement that spoke their language, that rekindled the embers of an American tradition they felt was being extinguished. This connectedness was powerfully emotive and politically mobilizing.

As these symbols and the invocation of the Constitution became ubiquitous with the Tea Party, they provided a template for political engagement that would echo into the future. The reliance on evocative imagery and the sanctity of founding principles would serve as a precursor to the Trump era's use of similarly charged rhetoric and iconography.

The connection between the Constitution and modern legislative efforts manifested in various ways, from challenging the Affordable Care Act to questioning the legitimacy of policies on taxation and governmental control. This interpretative dance around the Constitution set the stage for future policy battles and political standoffs.

What we can observe is a lineage, a clear transmission of fervent constitutionalism that would inform the strategies and temperament of the Trump campaign and presidency. The political scenery was changing, and the Tea Party had sown the seeds of a populist, constitutionally anchored revolution.

However, as history has repeatedly shown, symbols and slogans can be double-edged swords. They can unite and inspire, but also divide and misconstrue. The Tea Party's commitment to its guiding symbols and the Constitution would solidify their place in the narrative of American conservatism, yet the legacy of such fervor brings both celebration and scrutiny.

As the Tea Party movement blazed its trail through American political life, its slogans, symbols, and constitutional rallying points didn't just contribute to the genesis of a movement, they became an integral part of its DNA—forming a bridge from the tri-cornered hats of the past to the red "Make America Great Again" caps that would come to define a new era.

Chapter 2:
Ideology and Impact of the Tea Party

As the dust settled on the spirited town halls and patriotic parades just a chapter ago, a stark clarification of ideology seemed to anchor the surging Tea Party movement. In the heated climate of American politics, voices from across the nation heralded a call for a return to what they saw as the core values of America: limited government, fiscal responsibility, and an enduring reverence for the Constitution. The Tea Party, as it gathered momentum, wasn't just a fleeting tempest in the political teapot; it was a storm powering a conservative reawakening.

Diving into the crux of the Tea Party's political philosophy requires an understanding that the movement was more than a coalition of the discontented. It surfaced as an amalgamation of libertarian ideals with a conservative agenda, hearkening back to the founders' vision—albeit, a vision seen through a highly partisan lens. The core values emphasized weren't just talking points; they became battle cries for an entire segment of the population who felt their nation was adrift.

Limited government and fiscal conservatism were not merely abstract concepts to those waving the Gadsden flag; they were principles as tangible as the taxes they protested. In a climate of escalating national debt and government bailouts, the Tea Party harnessed the collective disquiet into a focused beam of political activism. Government, in their eyes, was too big, too intrusive, and needed to be restrained—its fiscal appetite curbed to ensure liberty and prosperity for future generations.

However, it wasn't solely the economics of tax and spend that the Tea Party aimed to influence. While fiscal matters were undeniably the engine of their dissent, social issues too found a place in the movement's tapestry. They advocated for an adherence to conservative values, often taking hardline stances on immigration, gun rights, and healthcare reform. It was this dedication to grassroots activism, this belief in the right and responsibility of the common citizen to shape governance, that lent the movement its fervent dynamism.

The influence of the Tea Party, of course, was not confined to protest grounds or the op-ed pages of sympathetic news outlets. The movement's true impact was felt in the halls of power, where the sheer force of their voters' will brought long-standing political giants to their knees and elevated mavericks who pledged fealty to the Tea Party's cause. Compromise became a dirty word to the purists, and "primarying" a warning to any incumbent deemed too tepid in their conservatism.

What might seem utopian to some—this return to a perceived constitutional Eden—held dystopian undertones to others. For every believer in tax cuts and deregulation, there were those who saw in the Tea Party an uncompromising force that threatened to erode the middle ground necessary for the functioning of a pluralistic society.

In sum, the ideological moorings of the Tea Party were more than an intellectual exercise. They mobilized a segment of America that felt left behind by the system, impacting the political landscape in ways that no one could have initially imagined. This chapter does not delve into the legislative struggles or dissect policy nuances—that is a tale for the subsequent chapters. Rather, it firmly places the spotlight on the creed that lit the fire of one of the most influential political movements in recent memory, setting the stage for what would ultimately unfold as the Trump era.

To understand the Tea Party's legacy, and its seamless segue into the political playbook spun by Donald Trump, one must first grapple with the ideals that crystallized under the banner of this populist uprising. For as we turn the page to subsequent chapters, the foundations laid here are the bedrock upon which a political revolution was built, a precursor to the seismic shifts that would shake the corridors of power in Washington and beyond.

Political Philosophy and Core Values

The Tea Party, since its meteoric rise in the late 2000s, has been more than just a political movement; it signifies a profound ideological crusade centering on a particular envisioning of the American political ethos that cascades into tangible policy stances. The political philosophy of the Tea Party, rooted deeply in the annals of American constitutionalism, is an invocation of the past to reshape the present.

Harboring a staunch commitment to the principles enshrined within the Constitution, the Tea Party seeks a rigorously originalist interpretation of this historic document. It's a vision painted in the shades of limited government, wary of overreach, and vigilantly guarded state sovereignty. They champion an America where economic liberty isn't shadowed by the expansive reach of federal mandates but thrives under a laissez-faire ethos.

This philosophy spills into a robust advocacy for fiscal conservatism. Tea Party supporters are often seen railing against perceived financial imprudence, unfettered government spending, and the specter of a burgeoning national debt. In their view, economic solvency is the lifeblood of national prosperity, and thus, stringent budgetary measures become a rallying cry.

Yet, while their economic principles are clear, the Tea Party's stance on social issues presents a more nuanced discourse. Social conservatism finds a place in many of the movement's platforms, though the intensity of those beliefs can vary across the spectrum of Tea Party affiliates. Some members emphasize tradition and social values as bedrocks for policy, while others fixate predominantly on the economic dimensions of governance.

It's important to understand that the core values of the Tea Party don't manifest simply as a set of beliefs or policy positions; these are the cornerstones of a virulent form of grassroots activism that has reshaped the political landscape. Their activism isn't just seen and heard; it permeates through every level of government, from local school boards to the hallowed halls of Congress. An unyielding commitment to see their philosophies reflected in governance drives Tea Party supporters to exert unprecedented influence on the political process.

Their uncompromising nature has both fortified their base and alienated moderates. For advocates, this fortitude exemplifies the American spirit of standing firm in one's convictions. For critics, it's a harbinger of deep ideological divisions that challenge the very fabric of bipartisan cooperation. Regardless, their impact is indelible, setting a course that reverberates through the era of Trump and beyond.

The Tea Party's fusion of historical reverence and modern-day activism evokes a sense of Utopian pursuit for its adherents—a zeal for returning to the perceived purity of America's constitutional roots. Yet, this same zeal casts a dystopian shadow across the aisle, feeding into a narrative of conflict and division. This dichotomy is a fundamental characteristic of the movement's political philosophy and core values, defining its legacy and undoubtedly shaping its role in the age of Trump. In undeniably clear terms, the Tea Party's political philosophy isn't just a footnote in American history, it's a chapter that continues to write itself into the fabric of our nation's political discourse.

Limited Government and Fiscal Conservatism The Tea Party's arrival onto the political landscape signaled a reinvigoration of certain philosophical axioms, centered on the ideal of a limited government with restrained fiscal power. Throngs of Americans rallied to this cause, aghast at the ballooning national debt and the specter of government overreach.

The core underpinning of the Tea Party's stance on limited government was the conviction that the federal government should adhere strictly to the powers enumerated in the Constitution. They saw every unwarranted extension of government influence as an encroachment upon individual liberty and free enterprise. This perspective was not only a call to action but a clarion call for the reclamation of a government of the people, by the people, for the people.

Embedded in the ideology of fiscal conservatism is the belief that balanced budgets and government efficiency are paramount. Advocates promoted the idea that just as households must live within their means, so too must the government. Consequently, the Tea Party demanded stark reductions in federal spending and significant reforms of entitlement programs as a bulwark against a future mired in fiscal insolvency.

Adherents to this movement laid blame on both Republican and Democratic administrations for the quagmire of national debt. Their argument was bipartisan negligence had led to reckless spending. Their solution was a return to frugality and the exacting scrutiny of every dollar flowing through the government's coffers.

The Tea Party's fiscal conservatism extended beyond mere budgetary concerns. It was an ethos that espoused the virtues of the free market and the perils of excessive regulation. Entrepreneurs and small businesses were to be the champions of economic growth, unleashed by the reduction of red tape and liberated from the heavy hand of bureaucratic meddling.

This economic doctrine postulated that lower taxes would lead to greater investment and consumer spending, fueling job creation and a more vibrant economy. The Tea Party was instrumental in propagating the belief that tax relief for the middle class and deregulation were necessary to rejuvenate America's economic prowess.

Austerity measures were viewed not as an end in themselves but as a means to achieve a more ignitable economic environment, where the spark of American ingenuity could flourish without constraint. Such fervor for fiscal restraint became the hallmark of Tea Party-backed candidates, who pledged to decimate budget deficits and curtail the scope of government programs.

The public's reception to these ideas was a potent mix of enthusiasm and skepticism. On one hand, the clarion call for fiscal sanity resonated with taxpayers disillusioned with government waste. On the other, the proposed cuts to beloved programs like Social Security and Medicare provoked anxiety among those who depended on them.

Within the legislative halls of power, the Tea Party's fiscal conservatism took shape through policy proposals that were both praised and decried. Some saw them as essential surgery to prevent fiscal collapse, while others decried them as cruel and myopic, stripping away a safety net from the neediest to feed the appetites of the wealthy.

The discourse sparked by the Tea Party's tenets of limited government and fiscal conservatism became a fulcrum around which the subsequent political battles of the era pivoted. These ideals laid the groundwork for the later policies and ambitions of the Trump campaign and administration, which sought to redefine the relationship between the individual, the economy, and the state.

President Trump's rhetoric, while distinct from the Tea Party's, captured a similar dissatisfaction with the status quo. The cry to "Drain the Swamp" echoed the Tea Party's disdain for what they perceived as a bloated and corrupt establishment.

While the Tea Party focused squarely on economic issues, the Trump era conflated these with broader social and cultural grievances. However inadvertent, this expansion of the political battlefield owed its provenance, in part, to the foundation of limited government that the Tea Party staunchly advocated for.

The Tea Party's insistence on fiscal conservatism did more than etch itself into the Republican Party's dogma. It created a ripple effect that would influence the tone and tenor of national debate for years to come, highlighting the ever-present tension between governance and liberty.

In practice, the Trump administration's adherence to fiscal conservatism was a complex mosaic. Tax cuts were delivered, but spending was not significantly curtailed, leading to critiques that the administration echoed the Tea Party's vocal concerns but not their rigorous discipline.

The dialogue championed by the Tea Party continues to resonate through American politics, its echoes shaping not only the Trump era but the discourse that will influence the path forward for a country ever wrestling with the scale and scope of its government.

Social Issues and Grassroots Activism When one peers into the swell of grassroots activism that bolstered the Tea Party movement, it becomes clear that social issues were deeply entwined with its ascendancy. The Tea Party tapped into a vein of discontent that transcended mere economic anxiety, straddling contentious areas such as immigration, gun rights, and cultural norms. These hot-button topics galvanized a base of activists eager to challenge the perceived erosion of American values.

The Tea Party's emergence can be traced back to its fervent advocacy for smaller government and fiscal conservatism, yet it can't be overlooked that its growth was also fueled by the passionate outcry on social issues. As proponents of the movement canvassed neighborhoods, organized rallies, and flooded town hall meetings, a common refrain was the desire to take back America. This mantra wasn't solely a call for financial prudence but a battle cry against changes to the societal status quo.

On the front lines of this crusade were everyday citizens, not career politicians or seasoned activists. The grassroots nature of the Tea Party facilitated a platform where the opinions and beliefs of ordinary Americans could resonate nationally. Central to this were the themes of patriotism and a stringent interpretation of the Constitution, which many in the movement believed was under threat.

Crucially, the Tea Party's strategists harnessed social media and digital communication to propagate their message, fundamentally understanding the power of the internet in rallying support and coordinating action. This marked a departure from traditional mobilization tactics and underscored a tech-savvy approach to political engagement, further exemplifying the movement's contemporary significance.

Abortion was among the social issues that the Tea Party had strong opinions on, with many of its members holding pro-life stances. This divisive subject drew lines in the sand not just between the Tea Party and its adversaries but within the Republican Party itself, spurring the emergence of a more socially conservative bloc determined to unwind Roe v. Wade.

Immigration reform similarly acted as a crucible for the Tea Party. Fierce opposition to what they deemed as lax immigration policies galvanized a segment of the population that felt unheard. The call for securing America's borders became as much a symbolic defense of cultural identity as it was a policy position. This stance against illegal immigration struck a chord that reverberated all the way to Trump's administration, foreshadowing his own hardline approach.

Education reform, too, became a theater of war in the battleground of social issues, with the Tea Party ardently opposing what they perceived as federal overreach into local schooling. This manifested in opposition to the Common Core standards, seen as a homogenization of educational content that stripped away states' rights to individualize curriculum.

The Second Amendment was yet another rallying point, with the Tea Party emerging as stalwart defenders of gun ownership rights. In the face of tragedies that prompted national conversations about gun control, the movement stood unwavering in its advocacy for the constitutional right to bear arms, drawing fervent support from like-minded citizens.

While fiscal conservatism served as the foundation stone of the Tea Party, it was the robust engagement with social issues like the aforementioned that deepened the movement's roots in American political discourse. It was this deft balancing of economic with social concerns that commanded a diverse following, capable of impactful political intervention.

This blend of issues created a tapestry that, while divisive, also formed a coherent narrative that supporters of the movement could rally behind. It became a resilient coalition, not disparate parts, which could exercise substantial sway over the Republican Party's direction and priorities. It signaled a broader shift within the conservative landscape, heralding candidates that mirrored these complex concerns.

Moreover, the Tea Party's engagements were often marked by an undercurrent of skepticism towards the mainstream media, whom many within the movement accused of bias and misrepresentation. This created a self-sustaining echo chamber where alternative media outlets flourished, laying the groundwork for what would become a trademark of Trump's presidential campaign and tenure.

As the Tea Party's influence waned and personalities like Donald Trump took the center stage, these social issues did not dissipate but underwent a metamorphosis. Trump's discourse and policies reflected the concerns previously voiced by the Tea Party, albeit with his own brand of populist fervor. This inheritance of the mantle illustrates the continuum between the Tea Party and the Trump era.

It's also essential to recognize how the Tea Party's grassroots activism showcased a blueprint for future political movements, demonstrating how deeply-felt concerns on social issues can spur widespread change. The rise of President Trump can, in part, be attributed to the preparatory work done by the Tea Party in priming the electorate for a leader who promises to champion these causes.

Finally, the Tea Party's legacy on social issues and activism endures in how it established a playbook for political insurgency. By taking firm stances on social matters, and cultivating a base of fervent grassroots support, the movement set the stage for Donald Trump's ascendancy, embedding itself in the fabric of American politics and signaling a new chapter in conservative activism.

Chapter 3:
The Tea Party Goes to Washington

If the Tea Party movement marked the burgeoning of a new era of American conservatism, its foray into the nation's capital was nothing short of a seismic shift in the political landscape. The 2010 Congressional Elections served as the crucible for this transformation. Here, we delve into how this grassroots uprising climbed the steps of power, injecting its anti-establishment fervor into the halls of Washington.

Midterm Eruptions: The 2010 Congressional Elections

The midterm elections of 2010 stand as a testament to the formidable force the Tea Party had become. Armed with slogans championing limited government and fiscal restraint, the Tea Party's candidates tapped into a wellspring of voter discontent that had simmered during the early tenure of President Barack Obama. It wasn't just an election cycle; it was a statement, a refutation of politics as usual.

With startling clarity, the electorate signaled its desire for a dramatic shift. In the House of Representatives, Republicans, bolstered by Tea Party support, reclaimed the majority by flipping 63 Democratic seats. This surge didn't just alter the balance of power—it ushered in a new cohort of legislators fueled by Tea Party ideals, ready to challenge the establishment's status quo.

Yet, the Senate also felt the aftershocks. Though the Republicans fell short of seizing control, the gains made were significant. Tea Party-backed candidates like Marco Rubio in Florida stepped into the spotlight, embodying a fresh and uncompromising brand of politics, refusing to kowtow to long-standing bipartisan cooperation in the name of ideological purity.

New Faces, New Power Dynamics

The influx of Tea Party representatives didn't just alter the congressional arithmetic; it recalibrated the power dynamics within the Republican Party itself. These were not the typical freshmen legislators ready to take a backseat to seasoned veterans. They arrived with a mandate from their constituents and an unwavering commitment to their cause, often placing them at odds with establishment figures who perceived negotiation and pragmatism as the keys to governance.

The result was a Republican Party at once revitalized and ruptured. Leaders such as Speaker John Boehner found themselves navigating a caucus more fractious than ever before, with new members frequently taking hardline stances. Their impact was immediate and unmistakable, influencing substantial negotiations like the debt ceiling crisis of 2011. Here, the Tea Party's ethos of fiscal austerity held sway, marking both an ideological win for the movement and a harbinger of the divisive confrontations that would characterize Washington in the years to follow.

It's clear the Tea Party's march on Washington didn't just bring new players into the game—it fundamentally rewrote the rules. As the nation looked on, a narrative unfurled that would weave its way through the fabric of American politics, edging ever closer to the rise of a candidate in 2016 who would claim to 'drain the swamp' with a similar disdain for the political establishment. But that's a storyline that warrants its own chapter.

For now, we recognize the Tea Party's arrival in Washington as a pivotal moment, a crack in the foundation of traditional American politics through which a new kind of ideology poured. The movement's integration into the highest echelons of government challenged bipartisan norms and positioned the Tea Party as a formidable force, one whose legacy paved the way for a new era symbolized by the ascent of Donald Trump. As we move forward in this examination, we keep a keen eye on the origins, looking to grasp the present by understanding the past.

Midterm Eruptions: The 2010 Congressional Elections

In the scorching heat of the 2010 midterm elections, a political tectonic shift occurred that was to shape the landscape of American politics for the decade to come. Swept in on a tsunami of fiscal conservatism and a groundswell of populist anger, the Tea Party movement catalyzed a seismic reconfiguration of power in Washington. With the battle cry of reining in government and cutting back the deficit, Tea Party-backed candidates stormed the congressional gates, fundamentally altering the composition and agenda of the legislature.

The elections themselves were a masterclass in grassroots mobilization; local rallies turned into national campaigns, and discontent was chiseled into political clout. Voters, fatigued and incensed by the economic turmoil that gripped the nation, looked past traditional Republican stalwarts and sought solace in the promises of the insurgents. These new entrants pledged to dismantle the status quo, shake the foundations of Capitol Hill, and wage war against perceived fiscal irresponsibility.

It wasn't just about the numbers, though those were telling—a gain of 63 seats for Republicans in the House of Representatives, the largest swing since 1948. This marked the dawn of an era where experience played second fiddle to ideological purity. Bound together by shared core values—limited government, lowering taxes, and a strict interpretation of the U.S. Constitution—these newcomers were to serve not just as lawmakers but as vanguards of a new partisan paradigm.

Their victory was more than just a political conquest; it was a message that resonated far beyond the halls of Congress. It illuminated the fissures within the GOP, foreshadowing the tumult that would come. The establishment Republicans faced an uprising from within, as the Tea Party caucus became kingmakers and gatekeepers, challenging leadership, pushing the party further to the right, and setting the stage for new populist movements to come to the forefront in future elections.

This was not simply an electoral phenomenon. The aftershocks of the 2010 midterms signaled a reshaping of policy agendas, with rhetoric that once might have been marginalized taking center stage. The Tea Party's ascension laid the groundwork for the anti-establishment fervor that would come to characterize the next chapter of American politics, culminating in the presidential election of Donald Trump in 2016. The echoes of the Tea Party's battle cries—against immigration, against globalization, against the political elites—found a new voice in Trump's campaign, and later, his administration.

With their outcomes indelibly inscribed into the annals of political history, the 2010 midterm elections were not just an eruption but a harbinger of the tectonic forces that would continue to shake the nation. The crusade that began with Tea Party activists holding placards on Tax Day would ripple through the decade, setting the tenor for a transformed Republican Party. With an ethos steeped in disruption and a relentless drive towards a conservative renaissance, the Tea Party's influence would endure, its spirit reincarnated in the America First politics that lay on the not-so-distant horizon.

New Faces, New Power Dynamics As the Tea Party movement surged, the gavels of power in Washington's corridors were handed to, or sometimes seized by, newcomers with a different kind of political verve. The midterm elections of 2010 served as a manifest vessel for the Tea Party's ideology as several candidates, perceived as underdogs only months prior, usurped seats from establishment politicians. This chapter delves into the narrative of change that swept through Congress, examining the political forces at play.

At the heart of this insurgency was an unyielding push towards fiscal conservatism and a stringent interpretation of the Constitution. The influx of Tea Party-affiliated candidates into the realms of power disrupted the established political alchemy, introducing a potent mix of idealism and intransigence that altered the GOP's internal chemistry. These representatives brought with them a promise – to reduce the size of government, cut taxes, and challenge the status quo.

Dynamics on Capitol Hill began to shift as traditional power brokers within the Republican Party sensed an existential threat within their ranks. Senior members who had long navigated the subtle ebb and flow of political compromise found themselves at odds with the newfound rigidity of the newcomers. Freshly minted lawmakers, many of whom attributed their ascension to a public outcry against Washington's perceived excesses, did not mask their intention to redefine the priorities of their party.

The presence of these new policymakers is aptly evidenced by their early victories. Attempts to repeal the Affordable Care Act, though unsuccessful, showcased a relentless drive to undo the perceived encroachments of the preceding years. This obstinacy signaled a seismic shift: governance, from their perspective, was not about nuanced adjustments but rather sweeping renovations to the very structure of federal involvement.

As these new legislators took their oaths, it became apparent that the tenor of political discourse was veering toward the polemics of a passionate electorate. The impact of social media and the 24-hour news cycle fanned the flames of polarized rhetoric, oftentimes overshadowing the more complex and less sensational realities of governance. The Tea Party's freshman class seemed equipped, if not eager, to ride the tumultuous waves of this new media environment.

Financially, the Tea Party's thrust into Congress in 2010 was bolstered by a network of donors, PACs, and super PACs. Funds flowed with the purpose of sculpting a legislature in line with fiscal conservatism. Campaigns were bolstered by grassroots organizing, yet also by significant monetary contributions from affluent supporters who found their economic philosophies reflected in the Tea Party's ethos. These economic power dynamics fed into the public perception of a movement steered by common people, yet their propulsion was intrinsically linked to deeper pockets.

The demographic shift brought about by the new arrivals also sparked contention and eventual realignment within Republican ranks. Notably, many Tea Party politicians did not embody the image of a traditional statesman. They walked the Capitol with a blend of populism and antagonism, a stark contrast to the stately decorum typically associated with such halls. This brashness was not only tolerated but celebrated among constituents who felt disillusioned with the well-polished manners of career politicians.

With every congressional session, the Tea Party's new blood encountered the rigors of policy-making. Their ideological purity faced the complex realities of governance, from appropriations to international relations. For some, the compromise inherent to the process began to chip away at their initial ardor. Others, however, remained staunch in their mission, seeing any deviation from their platform as a capitulation to a system they were sent to overhaul.

One of the most profound effects of the Tea Party's incursion into Congress was on legislative tactics. The adoption of brinkmanship became a marked strategy, with showdowns over debt ceilings and budget resolutions. Traditional Republican leadership found themselves contending not only with Democratic opponents but with an internal faction ready to risk government shutdowns to achieve their goals. These strategic gambits realigned the notions of political courage and recklessness, often blurring the line between the two.

The ripple effects went beyond the walls of Congress; conservative media outlets began adjusting to the shifting power dynamics. As Tea Party principles gained traction, broadcast narratives became increasingly reflective of the movement's talking points. For constituents tuned into these outlets, the political landscape was dramatically reshaped, painted in the stark contrasts of right and wrong, constitutional and unconstitutional, American and un-American.

Throughout this turmoil, it's important to recognize that the injection of Tea Party representatives into Congress did not solely define the period's power dynamics. Their actions and rhetoric often prompted reactions across the aisle. Democrats, attempting to reconcile the new Republican obstinacy with legislative necessity, occasionally found themselves negotiating in a landscape that seemed to rewrite its own rules overnight.

Despite any objective appraisal of successes and setbacks, the Tea Party's presence in Congress unquestionably embodied a transformative force. Their legacy would be enshrined not just in legislative scorecards but in the deeper narrative of American politics. They heralded an era that lionized the outsider, the challenger to the establishment, the voice that refuses to lower its volume in deference to tradition.

As these new legislators planted their flags on Capitol Hill, they did more than disrupt; they invited reflection on the very essence of political representation. Was their mission a triumphant return to founding principles or a jarring departure from pragmatic governance? These are the questions that historians would wrestle with, and that political opponents and allies alike would have to answer in real-time as they navigated a newly reconfigured battlefield.

From a broader vista, the rise of these new actors within the GOP promised intrigue for the political observer. How would the institution of Congress adapt to or repel this insurgent mentality? What would be the fate of these Tea Party protagonists? And, perhaps most importantly, how would the creed they championed continue to echo in the halls of power, influencing American governance for years to come?

Chapter 4:
Inciting Insurgency Within the GOP

As the Tea Party movement surged forward, it set in motion a tidal wave of political insurgency that would ultimately crash into the traditional structures of the Republican Party. The narrative of political upheaval transcends the simple tale of underdogs against establishment; it touched at the very core of American conservatism and redefined its contours for the new age. This chapter explores the internal battle lines drawn by the Tea Party's ascendancy, and how it sowed the seeds of a larger rebellion within the GOP.

Fractures and Factions

The initial triumphs of the Tea Party activists weren't just about winning seats; they were about shifting power dynamics. Old guard Republicans found themselves juggling the need for party unity with the unyielding ideology of their new colleagues, who in turn had little patience for the slower wheels of established process. The push towards a more rigid fiscal conservatism and a return to Constitutional purism was often at odds with the more nuanced balancing act long-played by seasoned politicians.

Fueled by a desire to reshape and reclaim the Republican narrative, Tea Party lawmakers didn't merely occupy chairs; they transformed them. From Capitol Hill to local party meetings, a spirit of reform was mistaken by some as ruinous radicalism, while others saw it as the long overdue awakening of the American conservative conscience.

The Establishment vs. The Insurgents

The cleavage within the GOP wasn't only about policy but approach and attitude. The establishment, represented by figures comfortable working within the intricacies of political strategy and compromise, faced insurgents who revered ideals over practicality. Compromise, a currency of political maneuvering, was seen as complacency by the Tea Party's staunchest advocates. This schism settled into a protracted struggle for the soul of the party, one where every primary became a skirmish and every concession a potential retreat.

The insurgents drove their agenda with a vigor that rendered the political landscape unrecognizable to some. They weren't the mere consequence of the Tea Party's growth but rather, the flag-bearers of a larger ideological shift that looked to reshape the GOP's engagement with America's future. As the chapters of the party's story turned, it was clear that the insurgents weren't a passing anomaly; they were a demonstration of resolve to dismantle a status quo that had for far too long gone unchallenged within the party ranks.

With every committee hearing, every bill, and every election cycle, these insurgent voices grew louder, not just in volume but in influence. They were the harbingers of a new wave of conservatism that would redefine the GOP and lay the foundations for new narratives, ones that echoed long into the future and paved the way for political figures like Donald Trump.

In conclusion, the insurgency within the GOP that the Tea Party prompted was more than a political sideshow—it was a forewarning of the seismic shifts to come. It set the stage for an era where politics as usual found itself contending with the unpredictable and often unyielding forces of transformative change. The next chapters will examine how these changes took root in policy and governance, and how they eventually coalesced around the figure of Donald Trump, reshaping the future of the Republican Party and American politics as a whole.

Fractures and Factions

With the Tea Party's ascendancy within the GOP landscape, the tremors of an internal insurgency began to unsettle the Republican establishment. It was here, in these tangled brushstrokes of political upheaval, that lines were drawn in the sand, demarcating a burgeoning war within the party itself. What began with purist cries for a return to the Constitution and the enthronement of fiscal responsibility eventually splintered the GOP into an intricate mosaic of fractures and factions.

The insurgents, a mixture of newcomers and seasoned dissenters, brought forth a vision steeped in ideologically pure principles, unswayed by the established norms of political negotiation and compromise. Emboldened by a grass-roots dynamism, this faction viewed the establishment as a bastion of ossified bureaucracy, ineffective against the perceived overreach of government. With the unwavering belief that they were the torchbearers of genuine conservative values, the insurgents aimed to overthrow what they saw as a complacent elite. This was a party in the throes of redefinition, a party where legislative purgatory awaited those who did not pledge allegiance to its most conservative tenets.

On the other side of this internecine conflict stood the establishment, gilded with years of political acumen and an intimate understanding of pragmatic governance. They watched with a mix of condescension and alarm as the insurgents, fiery and unrestrained, breached the gates of their institution. The very edifice of their power was predicated on the ability to navigate the political currents, yet they found themselves in the riptide of a righteous revolution that disdained transactional politics.

As the disagreements between these factions intensified, the GOP became a microcosm of broader societal tensions. Lobbyists, donors, and political tacticians were suddenly compelled to choose sides or to find ways to quell the unrest within their ranks. The splinters that formed in the foundation of the Republican Party were not just about policy disputes; they were about the identity and soul of the party. Narratives were constructed, sometimes painstakingly, to accommodate or confront this political schism that sought to rewrite the rules of engagement within the GOP. This was a period not only of political cannibalization but also one of ideological distillation.

Throughout the chaos, the insurgents drew from a playbook refined by the Tea Party's earlier successes, blending anti-establishment fervor with a new lexicon that resonated with an increasing number of party faithful. From these fractures emerged the blueprint of a new political orthodoxy, one that laid the groundwork for the unconventional triumphs that would soon materialize on a national stage.

Few could dispute that these sharp internal divisions laid down the gauntlet for leadership battles to come. They heralded a tumultuous chapter where the familiar was uprooted and daring political insurgents carved out their own enclaves within the hallowed halls of the GOP. It was within this whirlwind of fractious energy that the seeds for a more profound, pervasive insurgency were sown—an insurgency that would culminate in the rise of an unforeseen political titan and a reshape of the political landscape for years to come.

The Establishment vs. The Insurgents As we delve deeper into the fissures within the GOP, it becomes impossible to overlook the tectonic shift that occurred with the rise of the Tea Party and its insurgents. This was a form of rebellion—not with arms and anarchy, but with the ballot and the brash conviction that they knew better than those comfortably nestled in the echelons of power. The Tea

Party's entry into Washington was not merely a nudge; it was a seismic event that threatened to fracture an architecture of traditional Republican conservatism.

The establishment, those seasoned politicians who had weathered multiple administrations and congressional sessions, was suddenly confronted with a new brand of political fervor. With limited government and fiscal conservatism as their rally cry, Tea Party representatives brought an inflexible ideology to the halls of Congress. As such, they were often seen as mavericks, refusing to play by the unwritten rules of political engagement that prioritized compromise and deal-making over steadfast adherence to principle.

Somewhere among the numerous committee meetings and legislative sessions, a battle for the soul of the Republican Party began. The insurgents were not quiet about their intentions; they vocally challenged leadership, targeted incumbents they deemed too moderate and pushed for a purer form of conservatism. They saw themselves as champions of the people, defenders against what they perceived as a complacent and disconnected political elite.

In such a polarized atmosphere, traditional Republicans struggled to find their footing. The establishment was shaken by the realization that their once reliable voter base had pivoted to favor these newcomers with a different, more aggressive vision for the party and the country. Their authority was questioned, their experience downplayed as an association with a political class that seemed increasingly out of touch with the grassroots.

This internal GOP conflict wasn't silent, nor was it without casualties. Every primary season amplified these tensions, the primaries becoming battlegrounds where the insurgents would challenge establishment incumbents in a bid to reshape the party's identity. Tea Party-backing Super PACs funneled resources into these intraparty contests, further solidifying the insurgent group's status as a formidable force within the Republican landscape.

Out of this maelstrom of political jostling, a narrative of 'us versus them' took shape. On one side, the insurgents projected a vision of a patriotic resurgence, of taking back a country they believed was being led astray. "Drain the swamp" became more than a catchphrase; it was an ideology that painted Washington insiders as adversaries of American greatness.

Establishment figures, on the other hand, considered the insurgents to be a disruptive force, often derailing policy discussions and fostering a divisive atmosphere. They valued governance, pragmatism, and a level of predictability in political proceedings that seemed to fade with each passing election cycle.

Despite their differences, both sides recognized that the electorate was evolving. The insurgents were quick to harness the unrest, galvanizing those who felt unheard and misrepresented by the traditional power structures. This adaptability gave rise to an era of populism within the party, setting the stage for figures like Donald Trump, who later took the insurgent ethos to the highest office in the nation.

Yet, it wasn't just about being anti-establishment for the sake of being oppositional. The Tea Party's initial surge centered around real policy grievances like excessive government spending and taxation. This insurgent caucus pursued their policy goals with a fervor that pushed the Republican agenda to the right, causing significant shifts in legislative priorities on Capitol Hill.

This reality brought about a significant question: Can the Republican Party house both its seasoned politicians and the insurgent firebrands under one roof? As policy became secondary to proving one's conservative purity, the task of governance became fraught with complications. The insurgents' unwillingness to compromise — their preferred strategy being obstructionism — led to standoffs even within the ranks of the GOP, let alone across the aisle.

The Establishment vs. The Insurgents narrative is, at its core, a story about power: who wields it, who wants it, and what they're willing to do to achieve it. As the Tea Party movement reached its zenith, it became increasingly clear that the insurgent wing was not just a passing phase; they were instrumental in shaping the Republican future.

Looking at the establishment, the challenge was evident: adapt or face obsolescence. Yet, it was this very adaptability that ushered in an era of politics that was more about personality than policy — a shift that the Tea Party's fervor had inadvertently set into motion. The insurgent's scorched-earth tactics were effective, yes, but they also opened a Pandora's box of populist sentiment that would redefine what it meant to be a Republican.

As we reflect on the journey from the Tea Party's rise to the Trump era, it becomes clear that the insurgent mentality had, in many ways, laid the groundwork for the political climate that allowed for Trump's ascension. The overlap in rhetoric, particularly with themes of anti-establishment and deep skepticism towards the political status quo, made Trump's campaign feel like a natural continuation of the Tea Party revolution.

Ultimately, "The Establishment vs. The Insurgents" isn't just a chapter of political history; it's a living dialectic that continues to shape the contours of American politics. Its implications are far-reaching, touching everything from the rhetoric we hear today to the policies that govern our lives. The Tea Party, in all its insurgent glory, didn't just nudge the GOP; it steered it onto a new course — one that continues to chart its way forward.

Chapter 5:
The Tea Party's Influence on Policy and Governance

As we've seen, the rise of the Tea Party movement represented a seismic shift within the American political landscape. But what has been its tangible impact on policy and governance? Let's dive into the legislative strategies that have borne the stamp of this profound political phenomenon.

Legislative Successes and Failures

The Tea Party's presence in Congress had an immediate and profound effect, pulling the legislative reins sharply to the right. Fiscal conservatism moved from being a mere talking point to a guiding principle, and deficits and debts dominated congressional discourse. The sequester, a suite of automatic spending cuts, can be seen as a Tea Party victory in their quest to limit the size of government. Yet, not all their fiscal endeavors were triumphant. Attempts to dismantle the Affordable Care Act, known colloquially as Obamacare, faced numerous setbacks and ultimately showcased the limitations of their approach within the complex mechanism of U.S. governance.

Shifting the Political Spectrum

Without doubt, the Tea Party introduced a new political calculus. Incumbents who once appeared unassailable found themselves challenged by Tea Party-backed candidates in primary contests, pushing policy debates to the right. Even those within the GOP who were considered reliably conservative were forced to reassess their positions, or risk facing the wrath of a newly invigorated base. This recalibration wasn't confined to Congress either; state governments under Tea Party influence witnessed sweeping changes, from labor rights to voting laws, reshaping governance in swathes of America.

Such changes were not merely ideological stampedes; they offered a glimpse into a utopia for some, dystopia for others. The Tea Party movement envisioned a government pruned down to its constitutional basics—a vision that thrilled as much as it terrified. Whichever side of the divide one stood, it was impossible to deny the marked influence of the Tea Party on American political norms and policy conversations. In essence, the movement didn't just tug at the ropes of power; it endeavored to rework the very fabric from which these cords were woven.

As events would unfold, the echoes of the Tea Party's ideals found their resonant chamber in the presidential politics of the Trump era—a signal of their undiminished relevance. Yet, as Chapter 6 will divulge, the visceral reactions provoked by Barack Obama's presidency offered the Tea Party a distinct adversarial role and solidified their spot on the political stage.

Legislative Successes and Failures

The Tea Party's arrival in Washington was not merely a change of guard but a seismic shift in political philosophy that attempted to redefine the role of government. As the movement brought in a wave of lawmakers wedded to its staunch principles, expectations were high for a spate of legislative triumphs that would mirror their electoral success. The realities of Washington, however, presented complex challenges that tested the Tea Party's purity of ideology against the pragmatism of governance.

Burnished with the fervor of fiscal conservatism, the Tea Party's legislative efforts were primarily aimed at shrinking the federal budget and reducing the national debt. The fervent zeal to cut spending often collided with the intricate machinery of the federal budget process, leading to standoffs and shutdowns that left the public exasperated. Nevertheless, the Tea Party was instrumental in the adoption of the sequester in 2011, a sweeping measure intended to automatically slash federal spending. This legislative maneuver showcased the Tea Party's ability to bend the policy curve but at the cost of creating friction and the potential for long-lasting damage to public services and trust.

Initiatives to overhaul the tax code looked promising on the surface, yet yielded mixed results. The Tea Party's pursuit of dramatic tax reforms were entangled in legislative battles that highlighted both their relentlessness and the limits of their influence. One cannot discuss the Tea Party's legislative engagements without acknowledging the ardent opposition to the Affordable Care Act (ACA). Their attempts to dismantle the ACA, or 'Obamacare', never fully materialized, culminating instead in partial rollbacks and executive orders that chipped away at the legislation's edges without uprooting it entirely.

The strength of the Tea Party often lay in obstruction—defying bailouts, casting down infrastructure bills, and resisting budget compromises—illustrating that their political capital was sometimes more potent in preventing legislation than passing it. This oppositional stance echoed throughout the halls of Congress, reshaping dialogue and policy priorities in profound, albeit polarizing, ways.

While the Tea Party made significant inroads into American political consciousness, its legislative accomplishments were often either pyrrhic victories or disruptive stalemates. Yet, their impact on the trajectory of governance was undeniable, serving as a harbinger for future populists and insurgents. The uneven record of legislative successes and failures thus provides a critical lens through which to view the movement's influence—celebrated by some as the righteous stand of patriots, denounced by others as the epitome of gridlock.

In the woven tapestry of the American political saga, the threads of the Tea Party are vibrant and varied, symbolizing the duality of their impact on policy and governance. Their legacy is a complex one: a testament to the potency of grassroots momentum in the policy-making arena, and an illustration of the tumult wrought by uncompromising idealism in the delicate balance of democratic governance.

Shifting the Political Spectrum As the Tea Party movement gained traction, its influence began manifesting in various spheres of the American political landscape. One of the most profound shifts was the alteration of the political spectrum itself. Typically depicted as a linear continuum from left to right, the spectrum suddenly grappled with an insurgent force that defied traditional categorizations. The Tea Party's ethos, stressing limited government and fiscal conservatism, catalyzed a reconfiguration of what constituted the mainstream conservative ideology.

Indubitably, the advent of the Tea Party exerted a pull on the Republican Party, coercing it to veer further right on economic issues. This displacement wasn't subtle; it was tectonic, redefining the GOP's stance on taxation, government spending, and entitlement programs. Long-standing Republicans found themselves facing primary challenges from Tea Party-backed candidates who accused them of being too soft, too moderate, or — most damagingly — too willing to compromise with Democrats.

The spotlight shone brightly on issues such as the national debt and the role of the federal government. Debates that were once confined to the fringes of economic discourse now occupied center stage. The new litmus test wasn't just one's beliefs in free markets, but an unwavering opposition to any perceived expansion of government.

Thanks to the Tea Party, balanced budgets and debt reduction weren't merely policy preferences; they became moral imperatives.

On the social issues front, the movement was equally transformative, although more nuanced. While some Tea Party advocates prioritized libertarian-leaning views, promoting individual freedoms, others embraced a more traditional conservative stance, endorsing issues like tighter border control and stricter immigration policies. These were the embers that would later ignite into the blazing fire of debate around national identity and American values as Trump ascended onto the political stage.

The recalibration of the political spectrum can't be mentioned without addressing the cleavage between the establishment and the insurgents within the GOP. The Tea Party's ascendancy was a twist of fate for Republican stalwarts who had comfortably navigated the channels of power for decades. Now, they faced the uncomfortable truth that their base was no longer content with the status quo, demanding a more combative approach to politics, particularly against their Democratic rivals.

Implications of this spectrum shift were felt not just in policy proposals but in campaign strategies and rhetoric. Candidates were emboldened to take stances that, just a few years prior, would have seemed excessively partisan or ideologically extreme. This could be seen as a precursor to the kind of populist messaging that Trump would later masterfully employ to clinch the presidency.

The Tea Party's narrative around "taking back the country" and its critique of so-called "career politicians" resonated differently with various segments of the electorate. For some, it was a rallying cry for a return to a conservative utopia where government intrusion was minimal — a yearning for an idealized past or a path to a dystopian future where government has no role in leveling the playing field.

The ability of the Tea Party to mainstream once-fringe viewpoints created a ripple effect throughout conservative politics and beyond. This was seen in the willingness of Republicans to engage in brinksmanship, most notably during the debt ceiling crises of the early 2010s. Such confrontations were historically unlikely but became a hallmark of the new doggedness imbued within the party by the Tea Party's influence.

As this new political alignment took hold, it impacted the tactics employed by party leadership. Compromise became a dirty word, as the Tea Party's adherence to principles over practicality often resulted in legislative gridlocks. The implications for governance were significant, as the willingness to "shut it all down" over ideological differences marked a departure from more traditional legislative negotiation tactics.

An increasingly polarized political environment had begun to emerge, fueled by the Tea Party's insistent push to the right. This polarization affected the very fabric of political dialogue in the United States. Where once politicians might have reached across the aisle, they now found a chasm widened by the demands of a base invigorated and empowered by the Tea Party's unwavering positions.

Though the Tea Party era can be seen as a discrete period during which certain political dynamics were amplified, its lasting impact on the Republican Party persists. It laid a foundation on which Donald Trump would build his presidential campaign. The Tea Party didn't just shift the political spectrum; it sculpted a new one where voices once marginalized for their radicalism became central to the party's identity.

In the grander tapestry of American politics, the Tea Party did more than nudge the needle on the ideological dial. It spun the dial forcefully, expanding the bounds of what was considered politically acceptable within one of the nation's two major parties. And as the

Tea Party's influence began to wane as an organized movement, its legacy only grew stronger as its philosophy continued to percolate throughout the right, culminating in the success of Trump and his unique brand of politics.

Scrutinizing this change reveals an essential truth about American political culture: it is not immutable. It's subject to the forces of passionate groups that, with the right mix of timing, message, and media savviness, can redefine the realm of the possible. The Tea Party may have started as a small blip on the political radar, but by the time it had crescendoed, it left an indelible mark on the identity and direction of the Republican Party, having irrevocably shifted the political spectrum in the process.

In the final analysis, the Tea Party's role in skewing the political spectrum is a testament to the volatile nature of political alignment in a deeply divided country. As we map the trajectory from tax protests to Trump's triumph, it's clear that the Tea Party wasn't just a faction; it was a force — a force that altered the course of American conservatism and paved the way for a new, more confrontational era in partisan politics.

Chapter 6:
Barack Obama's Presidency and the Tea Party Backlash

In charting the Tea Party's meteoric rise in American politics, we cannot overlook the presidency of Barack Obama, whose tenure in the White House became the anvil upon which the Tea Party hammered out its identity. The chapter that unfolds here aims to analyze and understand the tumultuous relationship between the Obama administration and the burgeoning Tea Party movement, delving into the potent backlash that it inspired.

The election of Barack Obama heralded a period of significant change. His promise of hope and progressive policies captured the nation's imagination, but simultaneously, it stoked the fears and anxieties of a vocal and growing conservative constituency. Amidst this climate of division and change, the Tea Party found its purpose, becoming both a symbol and an amplifier for conservative America's deepest concerns.

Healthcare reform, widely regarded as President Obama's hallmark domestic policy achievement, became a central point of contention. The Affordable Care Act, or 'Obamacare' as it was pejoratively nicknamed by its detractors, became a rallying cry for the Tea Party. They saw it as the epitome of government overreach, an existential threat to personal liberties and the free market system. The movement's response was thunderous, a groundswell of opposition that capitalized on this singular issue to galvanize support and shape the national debate.

The Tea Party also seized upon a range of scandals and contentious issues that bubbled to the surface during Obama's presidency. From the ATF gunwalking scandal to the IRS's scrutinization of Tea Party groups, each controversy was fuel to the flame, used by the Tea Party to affirm their narrative of an overbearing and untrustworthy federal government.

Perhaps most notably, the Tea Party found resonance in questioning the legitimacy of Obama's presidency through the so-called "birther" controversy. This was not simply a challenge to Obama's legal qualifications but served to symbolically displace his presidency outside the realm of what the Tea Party considered true Americanness. The movement's fiery rhetoric around this issue showcased their ability to latch onto cultural and identity politics, entrenching deep political divisions.

In the face of these challenges, the Obama administration often found itself on the defensive, caught in a cycle of reaction and opposition. The Tea Party, leveraging a blend of grassroots activism and media savvy, established itself as an obstructionist force within the legislature and across the nation. The political strategy wasn't merely opposition for the sake of opposition; it represented a fundamental challenge to Obama's vision for America's future, setting the stage for a seismic shift in the Republican Party and the national political landscape.

The Tea Party's role during the Obama years was paradoxical. It is a testament to both the strength and fragility of the American democratic process—a reminder that activism can both stimulate political engagement and sharply polarize public sentiment. As this book endeavors to illustrate, these years served as an instrumental precursor to the political culture that ultimately gave rise to the age of Trump, with echoes of the Tea Party's dogged resistance woven into the fabric of America's ongoing political narrative.

By the close of Obama's presidency, the Tea Party had incontrovertibly made its mark on American history, shaping the zeitgeist in ways that continue to reverberate through time. This chapter, therefore, serves not just as a retrospective but as a bridge to understanding the intricate dance of action and reaction that underpins the ever-evolving tapestry of American politics.

Healthcare, Scandals, and the Birth Certificate Controversy

During Barack Obama's presidency, the tumultuous relationship between the Tea Party movement and the Oval Office was characterized by severe ideological clashes. Foremost among these standoffs was the contentious enactment of the Affordable Care Act (ACA), popularly known as Obamacare. As the Tea Party rallied for limited government, the ACA's sweeping reforms became a lightning rod for criticism—a symbol of federal overreach in the healthcare system. In town halls and on the steps of the Capitol, the outcry was fervent, with Tea Party activists lambasting the legislation as antithetical to their vision of America.

The administration also faced a barrage of scandals that fueled the Tea Party's narrative of governmental malfeasance. Incidents such as the Fast and Furious gun-running controversy, the IRS's targeting of conservative groups, and the tragedy in Benghazi served as touchstones for the movement. These were portrayed not merely as policy failures, but as catastrophic betrayals of the nation's trust. Each headline provided a fresh impetus for the Tea Party to rally its base, garnering support for their crusade against perceived corruption and incompetence.

Yet, perhaps no issue so keenly encapsulated the Tea Party's skepticism of Obama's presidency as the birth certificate controversy. Questioning the legitimacy of the president's birthplace became a strange bedfellow for genuine policy critiques—a breeding ground for conspiracy theories and alternative facts. Despite the eventual release of Obama's long-form birth certificate, the allegations persisted, asserting a fundamental illegitimacy of the presidency. It was a cacophony that reached far beyond policy disagreements and into the realm of identity politics, tapping into underlying currents of fear and nationalist sentiment.

Such confrontations during Obama's tenure were not merely policy disputes; they signaled a deeper schism within American politics. Healthcare reform, scandal reactions, and legitimacy challenges were more than fleeting events—they were emblematic of a burgeoning ideological war. The Tea Party's opposition crystallized into a vision of a nation at a crossroads, where the battle for the country's soul seemed to reach fever pitch. This rift laid much of the groundwork for the populist rhetoric that would later be seized upon by Donald Trump in his road to the White House. The question remained, however: Could the Tea Party sustain its momentum, or was it merely the harbinger of the polarizing politics that would follow?

Opposition and Obstructionism Throughout the tenure of President Barack Obama, the Tea Party's revolutionary zeal channeled itself into a powerful force within Congress, particularly the House of Representatives. The midterm elections of 2010 saw an influx of Tea Party-affiliated Republicans, many of whom had unseated establishment counterparts, armed with a mandate to challenge the status quo and to resist the Obama administration's policies at every turn.

The crux of the Tea Party's opposition centered on healthcare reform, known colloquially as Obamacare. This landmark legislation became the focal point for relentless obstruction, as Tea Party members viewed it as the epitome of government overreach. Their efforts ranged from legislative strategies aimed at defunding the program to challenging its legality all the way to the Supreme Court.

Observing the Tea Party's approach to governance reveals an inclination towards brinkmanship. The willingness to push the government to the edge of shutdown over budget disputes became a signature tactic. The fiscal cliff of 2011 and the government shutdown of 2013 stand as testaments to their unyielding stance against perceived fiscal irresponsibility.

Filibusters and procedural holdups turned into common occurrences within the Senate, shaking the very foundation of bipartisan agreement. By stalling presidential appointments and blocking routine legislation, the obstruction not only showcased the Tea Party's influence but also exposed the growing fractures within the Republican Party.

Debt ceiling confrontations emerged as another battlefield where the Tea Party wielded their newfound power. They infused the typically mundane vote to raise the government's borrowing limit with dramatic calls for spending cuts and reforms. These episodes reflected a dichotomy within the Tea Party—a juxtaposition of an apocalyptic vision of fiscal collapse against a utopian ideal of balanced budgets and reduced debt.

This tension extended to foreign policy, as isolationist voices within the Tea Party clashed with the party's traditionally hawkish stance. Skepticism toward interventionist policies and foreign aid further underscored the chasm between the insurgents and establishment figures within the GOP.

The ripple effect of Tea Party obstructionism extended to climate change and environmental policies as well. Agendas focusing on environmental protection were met with immediate resistance, often framed as unjustified regulations hampering economic growth despite the looming dystopian consequences of unchecked climate change.

Immigration reform also felt the brunt of the Tea Party's obstructionist tactics. The bipartisan push for comprehensive immigration reform was effectively quashed by Tea Party opposition, which viewed the proposed path to citizenship as amnesty and a betrayal of legal immigration processes.

As a result of these obstructionist efforts, a schism developed within the Republican constituency. The Tea Party's unwavering commitment to their principles attracted a devoted following, while simultaneously alienating moderate Republicans and independents frustrated with legislative gridlock.

The communication strategies employed by the Tea Party further entrenched their stance. Using incendiary rhetoric and apocalyptic imagery, they crafted a narrative of relentless resistance against an authoritarian government, fueling polarized discourse that reverberated through the halls of Congress and across the nation.

Social issues such as gay marriage and abortion did not escape the Tea Party's obstructionist agenda. Their vision of a return to conservative values often clashed with the evolving social landscape, marking them as staunch defenders of traditional norms in the rapidly changing cultural milieu.

Despite these divisive strategies, the Tea Party's unyielding opposition to the Obama administration served to bolster their influence within the GOP, setting the stage for the political climate that would allow a figure like Donald Trump to ascend to the presidency.

The Tea Party's effectiveness at blocking legislation and influencing party politics cannot be underestimated. Their approach to opposition not only shaped the nature of legislative battles during the Obama years, but it also perfected a blueprint for political obstruction that would be revisited in the eras to follow.

In the aftermath, many questioned whether this level of obstructionism was a constructive form of political engagement or a destructive force undermining the processes of governance. This debate still courses through the veins of American politics, echoing in the halls of power and across the political spectrum.

As the Tea Party movement waned, its legacy of strident opposition lingered, setting a precedent for future factions and movements that sought to amplify their voice through similar tactics. It's within this context that the rise of Donald Trump should be examined, as his ascendancy was, in many ways, facilitated by the path paved by the Tea Party's opposition and obstructionism.

Chapter 7:
The Decline of the Tea Party

As we delve into the labyrinthine saga of the Tea Party, we've witnessed its ascent to formidable political force. More than just a fleeting uproar, the movement's seismic shock to the American political landscape had pundits and politicians alike grappling with its grassroots power. Nonetheless, all empires—no matter how fervent—face the eventual prospect of decline, and the Tea Party was no exception. The narrative of its descent is both a cautionary tale and an illuminating prompt that examines the nature of political movements in the American democratic tapestry.

The story of the Tea Party's decline is weighted with irony; it's a tale of a movement that so vehemently championed the purist conservative mantra, yet found itself caught in an undertow of internal strife and external pressures. The shifting sands of public opinion, coupled with the natural cycles of political vigor, left the movement foundering. As its influence waned, many questioned whether the Tea Party had been a victim of its own success, co-opted by the very establishment it sought to disrupt.

Internal Struggles and External Resistance

Within the confines of any insurgent group lie the seeds of its own potential unraveling. The Tea Party, an amalgam of divergent interests loosely united under the banner of conservatism, was fraught with internal schisms. Disagreement over strategy and objectives led to fragmentation, and as its legislative impact fizzled, discord festered.

Contributing to these internal divisions were external forces resistant to the Tea Party's ascendance. The movement's reliance on incendiary rhetoric became a double-edged sword; while it mobilized support, it also galvanized opposition. Moreover, the very politicians the Tea Party helped elect faced the Herculean task of navigating governance while attempting to appease the expectations of an uncompromising base.

The Conservative Media and Public Opinion

An instrumental partner in raising the Tea Party's profile was the conservative media. However, as the party's struggles became more pronounced, the once cooperative narrative began to shift. The bubble of invincibility burst as these media outlets stepped back, recalibrating their message in response to the Tea Party's stalling momentum and the burgeoning new figures on the political horizon.

Compounding the dwindling media support was the fickleness of public opinion. The citizenry's enthusiasm dampened as promises met the immovable object of political reality. Moreover, the rise of novel issues and personalities began to eclipse the Tea Party's core agenda, redirecting the public's focus and further diminishing the movement's prominence.

Thus, we arrive at the dusk of the Tea Party's influence, a chapter closed not with a bang but a whimper. Lives were undoubtedly changed, and the political discourse was irreversibly shaped, but the relentless march of time tends to normalize even the most radical of upheavals. The Tea Party's once fervid embers now smolder, leaving us to ponder the indelible marks left upon the American polity, and the specter of what was once a powerhouse of change now absorbed into the annals of history.

Internal Struggles and External Resistance

As the Tea Party movement swelled, cresting with its significant wins during the 2010 midterms, it seemed on the surface to bear the markings of a lasting political force. However, beneath this veneer of success, deeply entrenched internal struggles were undermining the movement's solidarity. Members clashed over the core priorities that the Tea Party should champion. While some insisted on strict fiscal conservatism and shrinking the government at all costs, others argued for a broader agenda, including social issues and immigration reform, reflecting an existential tug-of-war over the soul of the movement.

Simultaneously, the Tea Party faced vehement external resistance. This opposition did not dwell in the Democratic aisles alone but emerged from within the Republican establishment itself. Long-time party stalwarts saw the Tea Party as upstarts yearning to remodel long-standing institutions and policies without due regard for potential repercussions. This outlook led to increasing conflicts both on Capitol Hill and back in the districts, where establishment Republicans waged a war of attrition against Tea Party candidates in primaries, pouring vast resources into campaigns aimed at quelling the insurgency.

Moreover, the movement's initially favourable coverage had begun to wane as media focus shifted to the fractures within. Compounding this was the evaporation of support from influential corners of the conservative media ecosystem, where once-ardent backers began to voice skepticism over the Tea Party's tactics, especially when government shutdowns and political gridlock seemed less like strategic maneuvers and more like quixotic crusades incapable of yielding substantive policy victories.

The grassroots nature of the Tea Party was both a strength and a flaw; it allowed for widespread and decentralized mobilization but made cohesive strategy and message discipline difficult to maintain. As local groups wrestled with their autonomy and the national narrative, the once-united front began to show signs of fragmentation. Inevitably, the lack of centralized leadership led to inconsistent messaging and priorities, diluting the potency of the Tea Party brand.

While these internal and external pressures worked against the movement, the ground beneath American politics was undeniably shifting. Activists who cut their teeth within the Tea Party began to set their sights on a new figure who promised to upend the system even more thoroughly than they had dared to dream. As the Tea Party's star waned, the stage was set for the rise of a political figure who could capture not just the imagination of the once-fringe faction but an entire nation, transforming the landscape in ways that the original Tea Party patriots could scarcely have anticipated. This backdrop of challenge and change within the Tea Party would serve as a crucible, out of which the mold for a new era of populist conservatism was being forged.

The Conservative Media and Public Opinion As the Tea Party movement waned and faced internal struggles, the conservative media played a pivotal role in shaping public opinion about its ideas and principles. The right-leaning outlets were instrumental in not just disseminating the Tea Party's messages, but also in laying the groundwork for future political shifts, particularly in the lead-up to Donald Trump's presidency.

Conservative media outlets, reaching back to the early days of right-wing talk radio, have long held sway over the ideological leanings of their audiences. The likes of Rush Limbaugh and Sean Hannity became not only standard-bearers for conservative thought but powerful influencers capable of mobilizing public sentiment. Their robust support for Tea Party ideals—small government, fiscal conservatism, and socially traditional values—resonated with listeners who felt alienated by mainstream political discourse.

Television, another bastion for conservative ideas, saw figures such as Glenn Beck translate the Tea Party's esoteric concerns about governmental overreach into captivating visual narratives. Fox News, the flagship of conservative television, amplified the Tea Party's voice, granting them a platform that often outshone those of traditional Republican leadership. The medium effectively harnessed emotions around perceived losses of liberty and identity, galvanizing a base increasingly receptive to outsider messages.

With the rise of the internet and social media, conservative web outlets and personalities further bolstered the movement. Websites like Breitbart News Network echoed Tea Party sentiments and later became fierce proponents of the Trump campaign. They created an echo chamber replete with discourse often untethered from the mainstream, fostering an alternative reality where the movement's rhetoric continued to thrive.

Digital media also allowed for highly targeted messages. Algorithms learned to feed users content that would confirm and intensify their worldviews, including the anti-establishment, anti-immigration ethos that had become synonymous with the Tea Party and would later be a hallmark of Trump's platform. In this online stratification of thought, conservative ideas fermented and evolved, unchallenged and unchecked by contrasting perspectives.

The result was a significant shift in public opinion among conservatives. Whereas once conservative thought prided itself on intellectual debate and the exchange of ideas, there was a noticeable pivot toward what some commentators dubbed "gut feeling conservatism." Emotions often trumped evidence, and media personalities who could stoke those emotions wielded immense power.

This emotional engagement was not without financial incentive. Conservative media outlets understood that anger and fear could translate into higher ratings and deeper engagement. Controversies were played up, scandals enlarged, and government missteps magnified—all to keep the base energized and engaged. And nothing engaged the conservative audience more than vilifying common enemies, from liberal politicians to so-called 'mainstream media.'

In the years leading up to Trump's candidacy, a fierce contrarian streak grew within conservative media, giving rise to conspiracy theories and dog whistle politics. When mainstream news outlets dismissed or debunked such theories, it only deepened distrust among conservative audiences. This distrust was weaponized by savvy media personalists who positioned themselves as the sole bearers of truth, defenders against a deceitful establishment.

As pivotal elections approached, the portrayal of the establishment—be it political, media, or intellectual elites—became an increasing focus. Conservative media successfully convinced a significant portion of the American public that these entities were not to be trusted. Instead, faith was placed in figures who, like Trump, promised to eradicate corruption and restore the nation to its former greatness, echoing earlier Tea Party slogans.

In this climate, the rift between the conservative media's presentation and public opinion often made civil discourse with opposing viewpoints difficult. The narrative advanced by conservative media bordered on Manichean: an epic struggle between good, patriotic Americans (represented by the Tea Party and later Trump) and their corrupt, liberal antagonists. This fundamentally shaped the attitudes and beliefs of their base.

The tailoring of conservative media content to appeal to feelings of disenchantment and disempowerment can't be understated. As the Tea Party began to recede from headlines, the same media that once gave it a voice subtly shifted their rhetoric. Emphasis was placed on the need for a leader who could bring about radical change, further setting the stage for Trump's 'drain the swamp' appeal.

As the 2016 presidential campaign unfolded, conservative media was in lockstep with Trump's messaging. Immigrant caravans, economic nationalism, and anti-globalist sentiments were regular talking points. The groundwork laid by years of Tea Party support transitioned seamlessly into a Trump-centric media narrative. Audiences were primed for a full embrace of Trump's politics, largely because it mirrored the ideologies once championed by their former grassroots favorites.

In analyzing the connection between the Tea Party and the era of Trump, one cannot neglect the critical role played by conservative media. By balancing the preservation of traditional values with the espousal of new political antiheroes, conservative media outlets shaped a public consciousness steeped in Tea Party ideology, ready to evolve into Trumpism. The bridge between the two was both ideological and practical—the media's strategy to appeal to their audience directly influenced the trajectory of conservative politics in America.

Ultimately, the conservative media landscape created a fertile ground for public opinion to grow increasingly dismissive of established political norms while embracing populism and a longing for political revolution. As the story of the Tea Party demonstrates, media influence can't be underestimated. It has the power to summon political tidal waves, leaving traditional structures scrambling in their wake.

Chapter 8:
The Rise of Donald Trump

As the echoes of the Tea Party's claims and demands rippled through the halls of power, a new figure began to loom large over the American political landscape. Donald Trump, a businessman of grandiose personality and even grander ambitions, would surf the wave of discontent that the Tea Party helped cultivate and would, against all odds, capture the highest office in the land.

The journey of Trump from reality television star to the Oval Office is as unconventional as it is historically significant. What began on the set of "The Apprentice" transitioned to the realm of politics, where he found a restless base yearning for the defiance of norms he came to embody. Trump's rise to power can't be discussed without recognizing how the seeds sown by the Tea Party movement prepared the soil of American politics for his particular brand of populism.

Trump's campaign capitalized on numerous fronts that resonated with the Tea Party ethos, albeit in a cruder and more unvarnished manner. His blunt talk and bombastic style captured the attention of media and voters alike, magnetizing those who had grown disillusioned with traditional political figures. Striking a chord with Americans who felt marginalized and unheard, Trump's direct approach filled stadiums, commandeered headlines, and ultimately, realigned the priorities and strategies within the Republican Party.

Furthermore, Trump's ascension was marked by a linkage of entrepreneurship to governance—a perspective that was often hinted at within Tea Party ranks but never so prominently wielded. Trump sold himself not just as a candidate, but as a brand synonymous with success and resistance to the status quo, drawing a stark contrast with his political opponents. Much like the Tea Party, he cast his narrative as one in combat with an entrenched and corrupt establishment, promising, in his famous phrase, to "Make America Great Again."

His "America First" rhetoric, while seen by critics as a retreat to isolationism, was, in Trump's rendition, a reclamation of American pride and power, appealing to the same constituencies that had once draped themselves in Gadsden flags. This nationalism, fused with a fiery demeanor, captivated a faction of the electorate who felt betrayed by globalization and ignored by elites.

As he barreled toward the presidency, Trump also imitated the Tea Party's broad brush critique of government overreach. He tapped into lingering frustrations from citizens still feeling the aftershocks of the financial crisis and healthcare debates. Trump's own iteration of populism, though cruder and often more divisive, promised a swift and decisive break from bureaucratic shackles, gaining him a following that saw him as a figure of change.

In dissecting the trajectory of Donald Trump's rise, it becomes clear that while his style may have been a stark divergence from the political norm, the groundwork for his ascendance had been laid. The Tea Party's revolt against the establishment and its calls for a return to a purer form of governance had cracked open the door. Trump, with his keen sense of momentum and opportunity, didn't just push the door ajar—he knocked it off its hinges.

In "The Rise of Donald Trump," the story is not solely about one man seizing the presidency. It's a reflection of the political climate he harnessed—a flurry of sentiment that had been brewing for years. This narrative is about a connection between a movement's fervor and a figurehead's victory, illuminating a pivotal moment in the continuum of American political history.

Apprentice to President: The Unconventional Candidate

In the grand theater of American politics, Donald Trump's rise from a celebrity businessman to the President of the United States stands out as one of the most unconventional and dramatic transformations in the nation's history. Far from being a mere apprentice in political maneuvering, Trump channeled the fervent spirit of the Tea Party movement to catapult himself into the White House.

As viewers once watched him on their screens decisively saying "You're fired," a certain segment of the electorate seemed to yearn for a figure who could impose such definitive action upon a government they viewed as deeply dysfunctional. Trump, with his brash confidence and disregard for political norms, appeared to be an avatar for this desire—a candidate not bound by the traditional chains of political correctness or establishment strategies.

His campaign was a whirlwind of controversy and unorthodoxy, sparking a media frenzy and captivating voters with his promise to "Make America Great Again." This slogan, though simple, harnessed nostalgic sentiments and a longing for a return to perceived past glories. It was akin to the Tea Party's reverence for constitutional originalism, igniting a similar fire in many Americans who felt disillusioned with modern policies and politics.

Leveraging his mastery of branding, Trump's campaign transformed him from a reality TV star to a political juggernaut. Despite a lack of political experience, his approach resonated with a base tired of career politicians and hungry for an outsider's intervention. Trump's strategic amplification of populist ideals and a tailored message to forgotten Americans cemented his place as a champion of the people who were desperate for radical change.

On the path to the presidency, Trump employed a diverse set of tactics, ranging from incendiary remarks and indefatigable social media use to massive rallies that galvanized his supporters. His campaign, rather than being derailed by scandals that would have doomed traditional candidates, seemed only to gain momentum in the face of adversity. This resilience appealed to an electorate weary of what they perceived as a brittle and disconnected political class.

Trump's success was, in part, an extension of the Tea Party's impact on American politics. Many of the issues that the Tea Party had brought to the fore—anger at the political establishment, perceived overreach of federal power, and a strong nationalist sentiment—were cornerstones of Trump's campaign platform. His adeptness at tapping into these currents demonstrates that, while the Tea Party as a movement may have ebbed in influence, the waves it created were still breaking on the shores of American consciousness.

The 2016 election revealed the potent force of an electorate feeling marginalized and eager for a political revolution. Trump's victory proved that the right candidate—one who masterfully harnessed populist sentiments and presented themselves as the embodiment of change—could dramatically realign the political landscape. His journey from the boardroom to the Oval Office was far from the path of a traditional apprentice, but it was a path that decisively demonstrated that in an era of intense dissatisfaction with the status quo, the most unconventional of candidates could indeed capture the presidency.

Populism and the Politics of Personality As the Tea Party's influence reached its zenith, the confluence of populism and personality politics began to take a definitive shape. If the Tea Party movement railed against the perceived excesses of government, it was Donald Trump's ascendency that personified this discontent and transformed it into a vivid political spectacle. The visceral connection between a leader and their base is far from a novel concept. However,

Trump's brand of politics harnessed this dynamic in unprecedented ways, building upon the foundations laid by the Tea Party.

When examining the surge of Trump, it becomes clear how the architecture of his political narrative drew heavily from populist dogma. He presented himself as a trenchant outsider, a champion of the 'forgotten' men and women, articulating a vision steeped in restoration and retribution. Trump's approach mirrored the Tea Party's antagonism towards the establishments of both parties, but his technique was more personalized, a testament to his unique brand.

In the politics of personality, it's not solely the policies that galvanize supporters – it's the individual's charisma and appeal. Trump's personal brand was built on the premise of success and defiance. Audacious and unapologetic, he inhabited a persona that resonated with voters disillusioned by traditional politics. This magnetic personality allowed him to take ownership of political discourse and direct it at will, with the promise to 'Make America Great Again' becoming a distilled expression of aggrieved nationalism.

Central to Trump's appeal was his rhetorical style, which often bordered on the incendiary and the theatrical. The reality TV star knew how to capture attention and reshape it into support, tapping into the vein of populace frustration a la Tea Party, but with added pizzazz. The parallels were there: like the Tea Party, he emphasized a strict constitutionalist view, muscular foreign policy, and a robust stand against illegal immigration. Yet, Trump communicated these stances combatively, ensuring they were inseparable from his larger-than-life image.

The use of social media in politics has always been a game-changer, but under Trump, it became a hyper-accelerated platform for cultivating personality politics. His prolific use of Twitter not only disrupted the media landscape but also created a direct and unfiltered channel to his supporters. Tweets became not just messages but declarations, each post a ripple through the traditional political establishment, much like the Tea Party had envisioned.

Populism often presents itself as a dichotomy, us versus them, and Trump masterfully wielded this narrative tool. He positioned himself as the vehicle of the people's will against a corrupt elite, echoing the anti-establishment sentiments of the Tea Party. But rather than diffuse responsibility across the political spectrum, Trump centered the battle on himself, embodying the fight and its focal point.

Furthermore, Trump's willingness to flout political correctness became a hallmark of his appeal, signifying rebellion against the status quo. In doing so, he fostered an emboldened outspokenness within his base, one that felt muzzled by conventional political civility. This brazen disregard for the norms matched the Tea Party's frustration with business as usual in Washington and provided an explosive outlet embodied in a single, defiant leader.

Correlatively, Trump's rise illuminated the risks and rewards of personality-driven populism. Charismatic leadership can expedite mobilization and create deep psychological bonds with the electorate. However, it also concentrates power and influence in one individual, eclipsing the broader movement and making it more vulnerable to the idiosyncrasies and missteps of that personality.

Trump's engagements – rally speeches, debates, and impromptu addresses – shared the fervor of Tea Party gatherings but were supercharged by the spectacle of his celebrity. His oratory brought out large numbers and inspired a camaraderie among his supporters that often felt like a blend of political rally and fan assembly, fueling a powerful sense of collective identity.

His economic nationalism, a pivotal part of his platform, resonated well with the Tea Party's emphasis on American exceptionalism and protectionism. However, while the Tea Party maintained a more purist libertarian streak on economic issues, Trump's approach was more flexible, appealing broadly to a base that felt economically disenfranchised and left behind by globalization.

The Tea Party's focus on grassroots activism was largely a principled stance against the concentration of power; Trump's campaign, however, transformed this activism into a fervent movement centered around personal fealty to Trump himself. This shift from an ideological to a personal nexus was critical in shaping the politics of personality that defined his Presidency.

In assessing the landscape post-Trump, it's evident that his persona-driven brand of politics didn't fade with his departure from office. The seeds of personality that he sowed have germinated a new crop of politicians who emulate his direct, confrontational style. This evolution bears testimony to the continuing influence of personality in populist politics, which was in many ways legitimized and emboldened by the Tea Party's insurgency.

Yet, Trump's journey also underscored an inherent paradox within populism. While claiming to elevate the 'ordinary' citizen's voice, it often paves the way for an extraordinary individual to amass extraordinary power. Populism can serve as a vehicle for genuine political change, but when married to the politics of personality, it underscores the fine line between a movement and a cult of personality.

As we consider the future of politics in a post-Trump, post-Tea Party era, the lessons of this symbiosis between populism and personality remain vital. They suggest a politics not just driven by grievances but shaped by the dynamism of leaders who can pivot those discontented voices toward their vision—exploiting the very human desire not just for policies but also for pageantry.

Chapter 9:
From Tea Party Themes to Trump's Triumph

The undercurrents of the Tea Party's rise within the American political landscape, with its clarion call for limited government and fiscal conservatism, were not simply ripples that faded into the calm; rather, they were harbingers of a seismic wave that would crest with the ascent of Donald Trump to the presidency. This chapter delves into the intricate tapestry of ideas and themes that wove together an era of political transformation where the Tea Party set the stage for Trump's triumph, aligning with the broader cultural and economic anxieties of the nation.

Immigration, Nationalism, and Economic Populism

The fervent dialogues on immigration that characterized the Tea Party's staunch advocacy for strict border controls became a central tenet of Trump's campaign. His rhetoric resonated, turning concern into a clarion call for a wall—a symbol of a fortified America, reflective of a burgeoning nationalism. 'America First' was not just a slogan; it became a doctrine espousing economic populism that promised the return of jobs, patriotism, and a redefined national identity.

Economic populism, rooted in the Tea Party's earlier distaste for globalist trade policies, found a champion in Trump. He championed the grievances of a workforce embattled by industrial decline and outsourcing, and his message hammered home the ethos of protecting the common worker from the exploits of the elite—a message that during the Tea Party's ascendancy laid the groundwork for this political pivot.

Draining the Swamp: Echoes of Tea Party Rhetoric

As the Tea Party demanded accountability and transparency in a government they felt had grown distant from the people, Trump's battle cry to "drain the swamp" echoed with familiar cadence. The phrase rang out, symbolizing the desire to upheave the status quo and flush out a perceived cycle of corruption and cronyism within the halls of power. This rhetoric did not merely encapsulate a political promise; it encapsulated a movement's ethos.

These echoes reverberated in the struggle to dismantle what many had come to regard as an entrenched political establishment. It was a message of defiance against the traditional guardians of governance, which became a banner under which Trump's campaign marched forward. His success was, to many, the realization of the revolution the Tea Party had long sought.

In dissecting the transformation from Tea Party themes to Trump's electoral victory, it is essential to consider the continuities in ideological underpinnings and the adroit adaptation of a resonant political narrative. The synergy between the Tea Party and Trump tapped into a potent mix of economic disenchantment and patriotic fervor, illustrating the enduring power of these ideas in shaping the course of American politics.

As the pages of history continue to turn, reflecting on this era, we catch a glimpse of a time when festering frustrations found a voice, when slogans born from a party of tea coalesced into a triumph that echoed across the globe. The question that remains is how, in the aftermath, these symbols and sentiments will continue to mold the future of political discourse and partisan identities.

Immigration, Nationalism, and Economic Populism

In the tempestuous transition from Tea Party tremors to Trump's seismic victory, there lies a trinity of themes that resonate with striking similarity: immigration, nationalism, and economic populism. This continuum illustrates a political evolution, whereby localized discontent over government overreach eventually burst into the Trumpian call for a fortified national identity and a retrenchment from the perceived excesses of global economic systems.

The specter of immigration loomed large, its presence in political discourse an avatar for concerns ranging from cultural identity to economic security. The Tea Party's initial forays into the collective consciousness of America incorporated a firm stance on legal and illegal immigration, leading to a disdain for amnesty policies. Trump's ascendancy amplified these murmurs into a roar, advocating for a tangible barrier in the form of a wall along the United States-Mexico border. The rhetoric shifted from simply advocating for stronger enforcement to a bolder declaration of sovereignty and an unapologetic prioritizing of American citizens.

With nationalism, the Tea Party's homage to the Founding Fathers morphed into Trump's "America First" doctrine. It was an ideological metamorphosis from a reverence of constitutional origins to an assertive stance on the global stage. This nationalist fervor under Trump questioned multilateral agreements and commenced a retreat from international engagements, a stark contrast to traditional conservative foreign policy that prized global leadership and free trade.

Economic populism, once cloaked in the respectability of fiscal conservatism, shed its subtler garments in favor of Trump's brazen approach. The Tea Party's cries against "big government" bureaucracy and deficits became calls under Trump for protectionist trade policies and economic nationalism. This inclination promised a return of manufacturing jobs and reprieve for the working-class Americans, a mantra that struck at the heartland with the force of a populist sledgehammer.

Indeed, each of these themes not only survived the ideological transition but thrived, shapeshifting to align with Trump's triumph. They underscore a narrative that the American political landscape was not just undulating but undergoing tectonic shifts, with emerging fault lines in national consciousness that would redefine the Republican Party for years to come. Whether this embodies a cyclical pattern or a singular political anomaly remains the subject of intense debate, the resolution of which lies beyond the horizon of current understanding.

Draining the Swamp: Echoes of Tea Party Rhetoric

In the political ferment that gave rise to Donald Trump, a refrain from the Tea Party's heyday frequently reverberated: "Drain the swamp!" This call to purge corruption from the halls of power tapped into a deep vein of discontentment that had been mined by the Tea Party years earlier. Wading into the murky waters of political stagnation, Trump's campaign latched onto this sentiment, recasting it with a brashness that appealed to a populace weary of establishment politics.

The Tea Party's influence over the language and tenor of Trump's political message is undeniable. Their rallying cry for smaller government and an end to the perceived elitism of Washington found new life in Trump's promise to dismantle the political establishment. As the Tea Party had laid the groundwork for a revolution within the Republican Party, Trump's ascendance represented the fruits of their labor, albeit in a form with sharper contours and a broader reach.

Both movements exploited a growing suspicion of the federal government's reach and intentions. The Tea Party's protest against the overreach of government interventions, especially following the bailout of banks during the 2008 financial crisis, was a precursor to

Trump's onslaught against the political class. He built upon their narrative, claiming that he alone could overhaul a corrupted system – a system the Tea Party had long accused of betraying the principles of the founding fathers.

But it wasn't just the message that Trump borrowed; it was the method too. Much like the Tea Party, he employed grassroots energy, though often through the medium of social media, to mobilize his base. This digital populism – a domain once dominated by the left – now became a tool for the right, amplifying Trump's call to "drain the swamp" in unprecedented ways.

Moreover, the Tea Party's penchant for outsider candidates set the stage for a billionaire reality TV star with no political experience to become the standard-bearer of the Republican Party. Their endorsement of non-traditional politicians who claimed to be untarnished by the ways of Washington smoothed the path for Trump's narrative of being a deal-maker unbound by political norms.

The anti-elite fervor was not just a playback of Tea Party themes but an escalation. Trump's contemptuous rhetoric towards politicians who had made careers within the Beltway resonated with a base that felt abandoned and voiceless. Where the Tea Party had been a cudgel against professional politicians, Trump's approach was a sledgehammer.

Skeptics of the swamp-draining battle cry noted that, much like the Tea Party, rhetorical flourishes often outpaced tangible reform. While Trump's appointment of industry figures to regulatory positions raised questions about the sincerity of his commitment to weeding out Washington insiders, his supporters saw these moves as a savvy means of leveraging insider knowledge for the public good.

Yet, this appropriation of the Tea Party rhetoric wasn't without its contradictions. Despite vowing to eliminate special interests, Trump's tenure saw the infusion of lobbyists and corporate executives into his administration. This raised accusations of hypocrisy, as the swamp seemed less drained than repopulated with different species.

Fiscal conservatism – a tentpole of the Tea Party – found a complicated champion in Trump, whose economic policies featured significant tax cuts but also escalated deficit spending. These deviations from Tea Party orthodoxy highlight the complex interplay between the two movements and underscore a broader dialogue about the priorities of modern conservatism.

The Tea Party's demand for accountability in government also reverberated through the Trump era. His administration's focus on deregulation and his support for measures that would scale back the bureaucracy was seen by many as a continuation of the Tea Party's mission to streamline and simplify government.

The phrase "Drain the swamp," while serving as a powerful rallying point, also underscored the limitations of political slogans. Transforming such sweeping declarations into policy requires navigating the very system that the movements seek to overhaul. Voters were left to measure the distance between words and actions, promises and policies.

As Trump's term progressed, it became evident that the swamp, as conceptualized by the Tea Party and later by Trump, could not be vanquished by pithy sayings alone. The structural complexities of governance and the entrenched interests of numerous stakeholders resist simplistic solutions, no matter how fervently they are advanced.

The Tea Party's echo in Trump's politics, therefore, was not just in shared objectives but in the shared realization of the challenges that confront populist movements. Both sought to reform a system they viewed as fundamentally flawed, yet both grappled with the contradictions and compromises inherent in their quest for change.

Overall, the endurance of the "Drain the swamp" mantra is evidence of its resonance with a particular American angst, one that craves the ideal of a transparent, accountable government. While President Trump adopted and amplified the Tea Party's rhetoric, his administration's outcomes spoke to the enduring complexity of translating slogan into practice.

In the end, "Drain the swamp" wasn't just a throwback to the Tea Party – it was an expression of a persistent American desire for renewal, a wish to reclaim a sense of governance that beans citizens feel is just and representative of their interests. Trump's embodiment of this desire ensured that, no matter the actual results, the power of the message itself would long outlive his time in office.

Chapter 10:
The Trump Administration: A Tea Party Manifesto?

In a political odyssey that unfolded with dramatic upheaval, the question persists: did the Trump administration embody the spirit of the Tea Party? As we adjust our historical lens, it becomes evident that the echoes of this formidable movement reverberated through the halls of the White House between 2017 and 2021. It's time to analyze and understand the extent to which the mantra of the Tea Party was inscribed into the policy and posture of the Trump era.

Certainly, the ideological synergy is hard to ignore. The Tea Party's clarion call for a diminished federal government and amplified fiscal conservatism finds its resonances in the Trump administration's legislative endeavors. Tax reforms that promised to streamline complex brackets and benefit businesses can be viewed as direct descendants of the Tea Party's taxation gripes.

However, while convergences are undeniable, divergences equally merit attention. The Trump administration's approach to trade, with its pronounced protectionist bent, signified a departure from the free-market chorus traditionally sung by Tea Partiers. This was no mere deviation; it was a defiant dance to a different economic tune, strung with strands of nationalism rather than libertarian tranquility.

Additionally, the pronounced focus on immigration control and the construction of a border wall exposed the raw nerves of national identity and security concerns. While these issues were present in Tea

Party discourse, the administration's emphasis was unique in its intensity and became a defining feature of the Trump legacy.

The impact of the Trump administration on the Supreme Court's composition is another facet that demands contemplation. The conservative appointments lent a judicial gravity to the administration's actions that could shape American law for generations. Here, one might see the most enduring impression of Tea Party ideals, as judicial restraint and originalism nudged the court to the right.

As we sift through these policy chapters, the underlying narrative is one that suggests the Trump administration both sipped from the Tea Party's cup and brewed its distinct concoction. Uncovering the layers of this relationship is not just an academic pursuit; it's pivotal in understanding the motors of modern American conservatism.

What's clear is that the Trump administration channeled the fervor of the Tea Party movement into its sovereign storyline. The result was not a carbon copy of Tea Party dogma, but rather a complex tableau revealing the movement's influence interwoven with Trump's unique political brand. This chapter digs deep into the groundswell of support that buoyed Trump to power, discerning how much of that momentum can be credited to the Tea Party and what it means for the future conservative agenda.

The spirit of the Tea Party, whether seen as a source of salvation or as a specter of discord, has unmistakably imprinted itself upon the Trump administration. This chapter isn't just a reflection on political parallels; it's an exploration of a pivotal intersection in American history. It invites readers to ponder over whether the Trump presidency signified a fulfilment, a mutation, or perhaps even a repudiation, of the Tea Party's revolutionary manifesto.

Policy Parallels and Divergences

The reign of the Trump Administration has often been characterized as an amplification of the ideals once championed by the Tea Party movement, yet there is much to be observed in the nuances of their convergence and rifts. At the heart of their alignment, we discover a shared devotion to economic nationalism, a spirited defense of strict immigration policies, and an unmistakable affinity for anti-establishment rhetoric.

Let's begin by outlining the unmistakable resemblances between the two. A hallmark of the Tea Party was its crusade for fiscal responsibility and a leaner government. When Trump took office, this translated into significant tax overhaul and deregulation efforts reminiscent of the Tea Party's desires. "Drain the swamp" wasn't merely a catchy phrase but also an echo of the Tea Party war cry against corrupt establishment politics, which materialized in Trump's executive orders aimed at curtailing the influence of lobbyists.

Turning to immigration, Trump's policies were seen as a reflection of the Tea Party's fundamental concerns over sovereignty and security. The notorious quest to build a border wall and the stringent measures against illegal immigration were policies that could have been ripped from the pages of the Tea Party playbook. Here, the ethos of "America First" represented a mutual thread uniting Trump's agenda with the spirit if not the letter of Tea Party doctrine.

Yet despite these correlations, it wasn't long before divergences surfaced, revealing areas where Trump's strategies and the Tea Party's purist views didn't quite align. The Tea Party's ardent pursuit of deficit reduction, for instance, contrasted sharply with the rising national debt under Trump's administration, fueled by hefty spending and tax cuts. For Tea Party purists, this was nothing short of a betrayal of fiscal conservatism.

Then came foreign policy. While the Tea Party held varied views, a common thread was a cautious approach to international engagement. By contrast, Trump's foreign policy, while isolationist in rhetoric, often took on a more confrontational tone, most notably with key trade partners and traditional allies.

This section seeks not only to pinpoint the similarities and differences but also to explore the contours of how two seemingly aligned entities can share a vision yet diverge in application. This is the complex interplay of ideology and practical governance, of campaign trail promises versus the thorny reality of policy-making.

In summary, the Trump Administration both embraced and deviated from the Tea Party's blueprint. The policies put forward by Trump often spoke to the core supporters of the Tea Party, reflecting shared ideals on economic and social fronts. Yet, the dissimilarities in governance, particularly concerning fiscal discipline and foreign policy engagement, highlighted distinct approaches to putting principles into practice. As the narrative of American conservatism continues to evolve, the interwoven saga of the Tea Party and Trump's era offers a rich tapestry of insight into the dynamic underpinnings of political movements and their translation into tangible policy.

Supreme Court Appointments and the Conservative Agenda
The ascent of the Supreme Court as a primary front in the political wars of the United States has unequivocally reshaped the contours of American jurisprudence. The Tea Party movement, with its fervent crusade for a strict constitutionalist approach, laid the foundational rhetoric that would prime the conservative base for the Trump Administration's judicial ambitions.

When considering the Trump era and its culmination of conservative efforts to realign the highest court in the land, one must recognize the strategic importance placed on the appointments of Justices Neil Gorsuch, Brett Kavanaugh, and Amy Coney Barrett.

Each appointment not only symbolized a victory for the conservative agenda but also served as a testament to the enduring influence of the Tea Party's doctrine within the broader Republican strategy.

The narrative that unfolded around these appointments underscored a dedicated commitment to altering not just the ideological balance of the Court, but to cementing a legacy that would outlive administrations and congressional terms. It was a forward-looking strategy, keenly aware that the courts hold the keys to long-term policy enforcement and legal precedence.

Gorsuch's appointment to the bench represented the triumph over the frustration that brewed during the Obama years, where a conservative base felt their values under assault. His nomination was a soothing balm, a return to conservative principles, heralded as a victory for the originalist interpretation of the Constitution that the Tea Party championed with relentless fervor.

The battle over Kavanaugh's nomination soon followed, transforming into a spectacle that polarized the nation. It was during this heated confirmation process that the conservative agenda was put to the test, with stakes that reached far beyond the walls of the judiciary. Kavanaugh's eventual ascent to the Court served as a rallying cry for conservatives, galvanizing a fragmented base under a unified banner of judicial conquest.

With Barrett's nomination came the opportunity to solidify a conservative majority that would shape the Court's direction for decades. It illustrated the convergence of Trump's populist appeal with the Tea Party's long-game strategy for judicial dominance. Her swift confirmation process, juxtaposed against a contentious presidential election season, was a stark reminder of how central the Supreme Court had become in the arena of partisan showdowns.

These appointments have become beacons of the conservative agenda, not just in the rulings they may influence but in the representation of a fulfilled promise to the Tea Party faithful. Trump's success in placing three conservative justices onto the Court underpins a strategic campaign promise made to a base that craved the validation of their constitutionalist views at the highest legal levels.

The importance of judicial appointments in this saga cannot be downplayed. They are the culmination of a vision that began with the Tea Party — a vision of a judiciary led by justices who would adhere strictly to the framers' original intent, thereby potentially reversing decades of progressive policies seen as federal overreach by the right.

These appointments can also be seen as a testament to the enduring power of single-issue voters, for whom the composition of the Supreme Court is their primary, if not sole, concern. This bloc of voters, who prioritize the Court above all else, was crucial in the 2016 election and serves to remind us of the importance of the judiciary in American political life.

The implications for the rulings that these justices will be a part of are vast. They have the potential to influence decisions on hot-button issues such as abortion, gun control, voter rights, and affirmative action. Already, the Court's leaning has manifested in cases that chip away at the bedrock of long-standing precedents, sometimes defying public opinion in favor of constitutional strictures.

In many ways, the success of the Tea Party in shaping the narrative around the importance of the federal judiciary has manifested itself through these appointments. Their ability to influence the discourse around the Supreme Court has ensured that, long after their protests have faded from memory, their impact on American law and life remains indelible.

Indeed, the historical significance of these appointments transcends partisan squabbles. It is a moment of reflection on the state of American politics, where the long game of court composition trumps the immediacy of electoral victories. It underscores a transformation within the GOP and the conservative movement at large — a transformation towards a judiciary-first strategy that patiently awaits the slow turn of the legal tide.

As the conservative agenda continues to unfold within the context of these Supreme Court appointments, the enduring spirit of the Tea Party lives on, embedded within the fabric of the Trump Administration's legacy. It's a testament to the movement's savvy understanding of political longevity, and its acute focus on the judiciary as the ultimate arbiter of their vision for America.

The lasting impact of the Supreme Court's conservative bloc is likely to reverberate through American society for generations to come, reflecting a confluence of ideology, opportunity, and strategic foresight. It signifies a profound moment in the nation's history, where the conservatives' judicial gambit has won a significant, though perhaps not final, victory in the perpetual struggle to define the American constitutional order.

Chapter 11:
The Lasting Legacy of the Tea Party Movement

As the tumult of the Trump era continues to reverberate through the halls of political discourse, one can't help but trace the origins of this seismic shift in the Republican Party back to the Tea Party movement. This chapter delves into the enduring impact of the Tea Party, not as a fleeting moment in conservative politics, but as an influential current beneath the surface of today's ideological tides.

The Tea Party's triumphs and tenets didn't dissipate as the movement's banners were rolled up and its rallies grew less frequent. On the contrary, the ethos of the movement has suffused the very fabric of the Republican Party, redefining its contours in ways that are both profound and polarizing. The shockwaves that were sent through the establishment GOP by the Tea Party insurgents of yesteryear have forged a new archetype within the party, one that would emerge full-throated in the form of Donald J. Trump.

Influences on the Republican Party and the Trump Era

The Republican Party of the early 21st century found itself caught in a vortex of change incited by the Tea Party. What started as a fiscally conservative outcry against government excess burgeoned into a broader ideological stalwart of the right. The grassroots nature of the movement gave way to a more confrontational style of politics that endorsed outsider candidates, eschewed compromise, and galvanized a base of Americans who felt left behind by the political establishment.

Donald Trump's ascension to the presidency was a direct beneficiary of the Tea Party's paradigm. He wasn't just the unlikely candidate who defied the odds; he was the living embodiment of the Tea Party's revolution against the status quo. His rhetoric of "draining the swamp" and "America First" resounded with the same fervor that the Tea Party had for shaking up Washington and prioritizing American interests.

Analyzing the Tea Party's Successors and Spin-offs

Though the Trump administration grappled with policy issues that sometimes deviated from the Tea Party's original script, the ripple effects of the movement's influence are unmistakable. Ideas that were once radical are now mainstream within parts of the Republican Party, from fierce immigration enforcement to a relentless quest for deregulation and tax cuts.

It's important to recognize that the Tea Party itself was not monolithic, and thus its legacy has been carried forward by a constellation of groups, each taking a piece of the Tea Party's doctrine and running with it. Some have focused on cultural battles, others on deep state conspiracy theories, and still others on an America-centric approach to foreign policy. Together, they comprise a fragmented yet formidable force that continues to mold the GOP's future.

The footprints of the Tea Party movement are indelibly etched into the landscape of American conservatism, with its sentiments echoing in the fiery speeches of populist politicians and the ideologies of a new generation of right-wing activists. The movement's spirit, albeit evolved and often contentious, persists as a stirring reminder of the power of grassroots fervor to shift the axis of a political party, and indeed, the nation itself.

As the Republican Party stands at a crossroads, it does so with the Tea Party's legacy as both a cornerstone and a specter—a testament to the movement's lasting influence and a prelude to the next chapter in the saga of American conservatism.

Influences on the Republican Party and the Trump Era

The contemporary Republican Party bears the indelible imprint of the Tea Party movement, an influence which reached its zenith during the Trump presidency. In this crucible of modern conservatism, the Tea Party's ideological fervor persisted as a driving force, one that promoted a profound reconfiguration of GOP tenets and contributed to the rise of Donald J. Trump.

The Tea Party's genesis in fiscal conservatism and limited government seamlessly intersected with the economic rhetoric of Trump's campaign. The clarion call to 'drain the swamp' not only echoed the Tea Party's disdain for perceived governmental bloat but also signaled a shared appetite for political insurgency. Commitment to tax reduction and deregulation, core pillars of the Tea Party, found renewed vigor in the policy agenda of the Trump administration.

Yet, it would be incomplete to discuss the Tea Party's legacy without addressing the cultural currents that coursed through the GOP during the Trump era. The movement's early days of grassroots activism had unleashed a steadfast critique of the establishment, sowing seeds for the populist insurrection that Trump would later harvest. His ascendancy can be seen as a natural progression of the anti-establishment sentiments the Tea Party stoked.

Social issues, while not originally a Tea Party stronghold, nevertheless gained prominence in the Republican Party ethos of the Trump era. Here, the connection is subtler but no less important. The Tea Party's initial focus on economic conservatism created space within the GOP for diverse issue advocacy, a space Trump used to court social conservatives fervently.

Furthermore, the Trump administration's engagement with Supreme Court nominations bore the mark of the Tea Party's original constitutionalist leanings. The advocacy for jurists committed to a strict interpretation of the Constitution resonates strongly with the principles vocalized by the Tea Party during its early rallies.

The impact of the Tea Party extends beyond policy into the realm of political strategy and rhetoric. The movement's embrace of blunt language and provocation laid the groundwork for Trump's unvarnished communication style, one that has altered the Republican communication playbook indelibly.

In scrutinizing the relationship between the Tea Party and the Trump presidency, it becomes evident that the movement's dogma permeated the Republican ethos, recasting the party's image and function. Trump's era was not only shaped by the Tea Party's ideological legacy but also magnified its influence across the American political landscape. The realignment within the GOP, sparked by the Tea Party movement, formed an integral part of the architecture for Trump's electoral success and the policies that flowed from it.

As such, the narrative of the Tea Party serves as a pivotal chapter in the story of modern conservatism. Its lasting impact on the Republican Party represents a fusion of activist energy and an embrace of anti-elitism, setting the stage for a transformative epoch in American politics—the Trump era.

Analyzing the Tea Party's Successors and Spin-offs As the Tea Party's fervor began to wane, many questioned the fate of its ethos and its role in shaping American politics. It is striking how the seeds sown by the Tea Party grew into a veritable forest of ideological successors, each branching out yet rooted in the same soil of discontent and demand for conservative reform.

The populist movements that have sprung up in the wake of the Tea Party carry with them a shared suspicion of centralized power and a staunch adherence to fiscal conservatism. Much like their predecessor, these groups advocate for a shake-up within the establishment, reflecting a persisting sentiment that has only become more pronounced with time.

One of the most significant successors to the Tea Party has been the Freedom Caucus within the House of Representatives. Formed in 2015, this group of lawmakers has been unyielding in their conservative stances, often pushing back against Republican leadership and advocating for strict adherence to the conservative principles the Tea Party cherished.

The ideology of this post-Tea Party faction, while resonating with the original movement's ethos of small government and fiscal prudence, has also been marked by an aggressive style of politics reminiscent of the grassroots passion the Tea Party exhibited in its heyday.

Another spin-off, though less formal, has been the rise of anti-establishment, populist candidates who have gained prominence within the Republican Party. These figures, exemplified by the meteoric ascent of Donald J. Trump, embody many of the frustrations and themes that the Tea Party first brought to the national stage.

The echoes of Tea Party rhetoric are conspicuous in Trump-era slogans like "Drain the Swamp." These catchphrases don't just encapsulate disdain for the perceived corruption of Washington D.C. but also reinvigorate a promise to return power to 'real' Americans - a promise that was once at the heart of Tea Party doctrine.

With the emergence of such successors, the Tea Party has proven itself not so much a transient anomaly, but a transformative force. Its offspring have continued to negotiate, often contentiously, the evolving landscape of conservative thought. This has catalyzed substantial policy discussions, particularly in the realms of immigration control, economic nationalism, and international affairs.

The landscape following the Tea Party has also included an array of media outlets and commentators who have built upon the foundations laid by the movement. These platforms continue to offer a voice to those who feel neglected by conventional politicians and echo the anti-elite narrative that the Tea Party mainstreamed.

Pivoting from strict conservatism, new populists within the Tea Party's lineage have ventured into realms traditionally not associated with fiscal conservatism, tackling immigration and trade with a nationalistic fervor that has reshaped political discourse and policy.

Alongside the stark ideological stances, successors to the Tea Party experiment with the role of digital media and social networks to organize and disseminate their message. This adaptation signifies an understanding that the battleground for political hearts and minds has shifted from town hall protests to online platforms.

While the newly emerged groups and personalities share with the Tea Party a certain do-or-die commitment to their vision of America, they also diverge in strategy and scope. They have proved willing to partner with broader coalitions, and to some extent, even moderate their message to achieve political victories and gain influence within the GOP.

In analyzing these successors and spin-offs, we must acknowledge how they have challenged traditional party lines and altered the political landscape. Their influence has been fundamental in the establishment of 'outsider' candidates and non-conventional methods of governance, as seen in the Trump administration.

However, the journey from Tea Party activism to the corridors of power has not been without its share of ideological dilution and compromise. The practicalities of governance have often softened the more radical proposals pushed by successors to the Tea Party. Yet, their ability to direct the conversation and sway policy remains evident.

The Tea Party's most profound legacy lays not just in the policies it influenced, but in the manner it redefined political mobilization and the expression of conservative values. Its successors and spin-offs continue this redefinition, ensuring the Tea Party's DNA is woven into the fabric of contemporary American conservatism.

As the analysis unfolds, it becomes clear that by understanding these successors, we gain insight into the perplexing and often paradoxical political era initiated by the Tea Party and catapulted forward by the rise of Trump. The movement's ramifications continue to ripple through America's political waters, leaving us with crucial questions about the future trajectory of conservative politics in the United States.

Chapter 12:
The Road Ahead: Trump's Impact on the Future GOP

As we transition from the Tea Party's zenith and its intricate webs within the corridors of power, we journey into a labyrinth where echoes of the past fuse with the clarion calls of the future. The Trump era has not only changed the landscape but has indeed carved out the contours of a new realm where the Republican Party now finds its footing. Donald Trump's presidency was both a progeny and a reinventing force for trends that the Tea Party pioneered, yet it also portends a transformation with enduring consequences for the GOP.

Trump's governance was an odyssey, unorthodox in its conduct, evocative in its rhetoric, and polarizing in its policies. With an unyielding grip on the Republican base, he captured the heart and soul of a faction that veered away from traditional conservative tenets towards an ethos steeped in nationalism and populism. This significant shift poses important questions: will the GOP maintain this trajectory, or will it pivot in response to the ever-evolving political theatre?

The Party Post-Trump: Continuity or Change?

As Trump's term concluded, a schism within the party was more palpable than ever. Republicans are now faced with a conundrum that is two-fold: embracing the magnetism of Trump's legacy while also reconnoitering the frontiers that may keep them in lockstep with an electorate in flux. Will the GOP's future follow the brashness of Trump's populism, or will it seek a return to the conservative roots oft-perceived as overshadowed by his brand of politics?

The looming weight of this question is no feather; it is a colossal anchor tethering the party's future prospects to the strategies they employ today. The GOP's adaptation to the road ahead may very well hinge on their willingness to either align with or distance themselves from Trump's shadow.

Potential Candidates and Ideological Shifts

Looking towards the horizon, the aurora of potential candidates vying for the GOP mantle is as diverse as it is intriguing. Figures molded in the fires of Trumpian politics may contend with traditionalists for the soul of the party, each offering distinct pathways as they navigate through the Trump era's aftermath. Therein lies the dance of democracy as the Republican Party grapples with ideological shifts and aligns its values with the aspirations of the changing face of America.

What stands immutable through this is the indelible mark that Donald Trump has cast over the GOP. His presidency remains both a blueprint and a cautionary tale, encapsulating the adage that the only constant is change. The Trumpian impact will palpably resonate through the Republican corridors, in primary races, policy stances, and national debates, setting a precedent for a future that is both uncertain and inevitable.

As the GOP stands at the crossroads of its future, the party's direction is not merely a choice, but a testament to the growing pains and evolving dynamism of American politics. Democracy's heart beats loudest in the throes of change, and the impact of Trump on the future GOP is thus not merely a chapter closing but a saga unfolding amidst the shifting American political tides.

The Party Post-Trump: Continuity or Change?

The labyrinthine journey of the GOP, from the brazen outcries of the Tea Party to the meteoric ascendancy of Donald Trump, has led to the inescapable contemplation of the Republican Party's identity in a post-Trump era. Will the Grand Old Party embrace continuity, or pivot towards profound change?

While echoes of Tea Party's insistence on limited government and fiscal restraint linger in the halls of power, the GOP, under Trump's aegis, grew to represent a different set of values—nationalism, economic populism, and a brash dismissal of the political establishment. As Trump's towering figure recedes into the political backdrop, one question remains prominent: What facets of his legacy will the Republican Party clutch onto?

The Trump era has enriched the GOP tapestry with threads of economic protectionism and an 'America First' doctrine—a stark departure from the Tea Party's libertarian streak. Yet, the core of the Tea Party ideology, with its emphasis on strict constitutionalism and tax reform, continues to find resonance among the party's base. Thus, while the stage may seem set for a great ideological reset, it's evident that Trump's influence permeates the party's modern identity.

Meaningful change does not occur in a vacuum; it is precipitated by a relentless wave of events, sentiments, and figures. In the wake of Trump, a slew of potential Republican standard-bearers wait in the wings. These individuals, each wielding disparate interpretations of conservatism, prepare to chart their course, positing a pivotal question—will they emerge as true ideologues, or will they, too, be shaped by the charismatic sway of their predecessors?

Thus, the GOP stands at a crossroads. One path leads to continuity—a reaffirmation of Trumpian philosophy, while the other beckons change—a return, perhaps, to more traditional conservative values or even the origination of an entirely new political synthesis. The horizon is rife with uncertainty, but one thing is unambiguous: the Republican Party's destiny is intricately bound to the choices it will make in the ever-evolving American political odyssey.

The permeating impact of Trump stands as a testament that personalities can, in fact, profoundly mold a party's course. Yet, it's the ideals and policies—the tangible manifestations of political will—that endure. As such, whether the GOP maintains its course or alters its trajectory, it's clear that the principles adopted in this moment of reckoning will unequivocally shape the contours of American governance for the immediate future.

As we peer down the twisting path that lies ahead for the GOP, we're left to wonder if the fusion of the Tea Party's rigorous conservatism and Trump's indelible mark will serve as the foundation upon which the party will build its future, or if we will witness an unexpected metamorphosis, propelling the Republican Party into uncharted ideological waters. Whatever the outcome, one truth stands clear: the ripple effect of Trump's presidency will echo through the annals of the GOP for generations to come.

Potential Candidates and Ideological Shifts As we've delved into the evolution of the GOP from the Tea Party's insurgency to Trump's presidency, it becomes essential to analyze the potential candidates that are emerging in the wake of Trump's domination of the political landscape. As autumns shed leaves in a premonition of the chilling winter, Trump's era too, appears to be seasoning with time— his influence remaining, but the stage slowly setting for change. Amidst this ideological shift, new figures embody echoes of populism infused with their visions, signaling a Republican Party in flux.

The Tea Party's values—limited government, fiscal conservatism, and a strict adherence to constitutional principles—have firmly rooted themselves in the GOP's soil. The span of Trump's presidency has seen these ideals metamorphose, now entangled with a heightened sense of nationalism and economic populism. Yet, the question lingers heavily upon the future: what ideologies will the next breed of leaders carry forward or leave behind?

As speculations swirl, it's impossible to ignore the eagerness of certain candidates to step into the post-Trump spotlight. They seem to be treading a delicate tightrope between allegiance to the former president and the crafting of an independent narrative—one which appeals to the base honed by both the Tea Party and Trump, yet pioneers beyond to new political heights—or depths.

In this vein, the discourse pivots to potential figures who may seize the Republican banner. Some, wearing the mantle of Trumpism proudly; others veer slightly, hinting at a recalibration—toward either a more traditional conservatism or a tech-savvy libertarianism. The cast of potentials grows and shifts like chess pieces on a grand political board, with each contingent on the volatile whims of an electorate reshaped by recent history.

Names buzz with potential energy—senators with presidential timbre, governors wielding executive experience, and an array of outsiders who promise to shake foundations just as Trump did. No corner of the conservative spectrum goes unwhispered—from the hardliners to the pragmatists, each narrative offers a window into an ideological shift that seeks to capture the imagination of a party in restless pursuit of identity.

One must consider the subtle deviations from the Tea Party's original manifesto, particularly in the realm of social policy. Once ardent proponents of socially conservative views, a chasm appears to be emerging—some candidates leaning towards a more libertarian stance, potentially appealing to a younger, more diverse set of constituents. Others double down on the cultural conservativism, seeing it as the bedrock of a fractious yet loyal base.

Arguably, the ideological purity test of the past has morphed into a litmus test of loyalty to Trump's persona. Candidates are sculpting their platforms with a keen awareness of Trump's enduring hold on the GOP. Yet, the perceptive observer can't help but notice the careful inclusion of distinct personal priorities that could quietly steer the party away from some of Trump's most contentious legacies.

Examining these shifts, one icily contemplates the utopian visions of a reformed conservative party, or the dystopian prospects should the pendulum swing too far. Commentators muse about a paradigm where the restraining principles of governmental limitation espoused by the Tea Party collide with the hegemonic appetite of Trumpism. The synthesis—or perhaps the struggle—of these ideas will be the battleground where future candidates prove their mettle.

Moreover, technological advancements and the rise of social media have shifted the strategy and outreach of these burgeoning leaders. No longer tethered to traditional media, candidates now directly sculpt their personas within the digital realm, creating an ideological battleground unfettered by previous conventions. The potential for rapid mobilization or the risks of public relations missteps are ever-present in this new arena of political discourse.

The undercurrent of economic discourse has palpably shifted as well. Where the Tea Party found stalwart ground on austerity and the merits of free-market capitalism, some successors hint at nuances—acknowledging the appeal of populist economic policies amongst a base that has felt the strain of globalization and economic dislocation.

In the aftermath of Trump's presidency, foreign policy too, has become an aspect of divergence. The hawkish interventions rejected by the Tea Party's libertarian wing have been replaced by Trumpian isolationism. Yet, as the world grows ever more connected, there are those among the candidates who quietly suggest a balance—a robust American presence without the overreach.

This stretch on the political spectrum, however, seems tentative at best. With geopolitical challenges abound, including the rise of authoritarianism and digital warfare, any shift in ideology must be carefully calibrated to ensure national interests are preserved while appealing to a base that yearns for simplicity in the complex web of international relations.

The slow rhythm of this ideological shift beats within the grander narrative of American politics. It is a tale of adaptation and survival, where the next set of candidates will not merely inherit the GOP but will shape it through the furnace of their convictions and the heartbeats of their campaigns. Each whispers promises of preservation and resurgence, of upending tradition or embracing the ghosts of Tea Party past—all while gazing upon the America they hope to lead.

As the Republican Party stands at this crossroads, the prospective candidates must navigate treacherous political terrain. They must weave between passions fueled by a former president's emboldened base, a Tea Party that catalyzed shift and shakeup, and the inevitable propulsion towards future electorates hungry for policy that resonates with their lived realities.

The murmurings of the next presidential election cycle converge with these ideological shifts in seismic fashion. Visionaries or ideologues, denizens of the old guard or harbingers of a new conservative renaissance—they all step forth, armed with lessons from the coupling of the Tea Party and Trump. As curtains draw slowly on one political epoch, they beckon to the next, pledging to recast the GOP in an image reforged by the trials of a turbulent decade. Only time will narrate the efficacy of these candidates and the ideological paths they champion, as the electorate waits, watches, and weighs its fate.

Pouring Over the Past, Projecting the Future

In the shifting sands of American politics, the strains of the Tea Party movement have woven themselves into the fabric of our contemporary landscape. As we reflect on the tumultuous years from the insurgent cries for smaller government to the thunderous rallies for "Making America Great Again," it becomes clear that these movements have not only collided but merged, shaping a new partisan archetype.

The Tea Party, with its fervent push against taxation and big government, had grown from a whisper to a roar by 2010. It was the year that saw a seismic shift in congressional power dynamics, sending shudders through the corridors of Washington. This power play redefined the Republican Party, laying the foundation on which a figure like Donald Trump would later stand tall.

Yet, even as we chart the course of the Tea Party's drive and influence over policy, the tally of their legislative forays reveals a tapestry of victories and setbacks. Through their lens, each legislative attempt carried the weight of ideological purity, shifting the political spectrum in a way that resonated deeply with millions of Americans. It was in this milieu that Trump found fertile ground for his brand of populism—a soil enriched by Tea Party rhetoric and tilled by their relentless activism.

Traversing through Obama's presidency and the barrage of Tea Party backlash, one can't overlook the healthcare debates, the scandals, and the specter of the birth certificate fiasco. These were not just skirmishes but markers of an expanding battleground between clashing visions of America's future. The relationship between Obama's tenure and the Tea Party created a reflexive response that bolstered their sense of mission—and later, it would seem, Trump's electoral playbook.

As the establishments collided with insurgents within the GOP, fractures widened into chasms. The Republican Party was not just engaging in an identity crisis; it was undergoing an evolution, or to some, a revolution. The battles within would reshape the party's persona, birthing a new cadre of politicians who now walk the halls with an air of insurgency.

The rise and subsequent wane of the Tea Party—punctuated by internal struggles and a shifting conservative media landscape—prepared the stage for a new act, one far removed from the array of tricorner hats but still steeped in the spirit of rebellion. This dimming, however, was not the end of their story but rather a transformation as the Trump era breathed new life into the embers left by the Tea Party.

The parallels between the Tea Party's aims and Trump's administration are striking—and telling. From Supreme Court appointments to forcefully articulated national discourse, Trump's time in office carried forward the conservative agenda with profound verve. Yet, the divergences cannot be ignored, for Trump's methodology and persona would often eclipse the initial principles that the Tea Party held dear.

As we venture to untangle the lasting legacy of the Tea Party movement, its DNA appears clearly etched within the Trump Era's contour lines. Analyzing the successors and spin-offs that continue to emerge, it's evident that the Tea Party's spirit has morphed into something both reflective of its origins and unique to our current day.

The road ahead for the GOP, in a post-Trump political vista, is laden with questions of continuity and change. Will the Tea Party's ideological legacy continue to nourish Trump's base? Can the Republican Party harness the force without succumbing to the fractures? The potential candidates already jostling for position will have to grapple with these ideological shifts and the specter of the past.

Projecting the future, it becomes clear that the influence of the Tea Party and Trump will not dissipate with time. Instead, it will continue shaping the very essence of party politics, candidate profiles, and policy priorities. The ripple effects will span far beyond rallies and retweets, embedding into the legislative dialogues and judicial considerations of tomorrow.

The markers we see today—the emboldened nationalism, the intense focus on immigration, and the rallying cry against the perceived swamp of politics—serve as signposts of the road traveled. But they are also beacons illuminating paths yet trodden, impacting conversations that redefine what it means to be Republican in this new age.

Now, as we pour over the past, a future is projected where activism interlaces with governance, and slogans crystalize into policy. The constellation of ideas that once seemed like mere points of light has coalesced into a narrative that will shape America's political journey for years to come.

The book in your hands is but a map of this journey, charting the terrains navigated by the Tea Party and the Trump era. As we look ahead, let it serve as both a chronicle of history and a compass for understanding the currents of our political tides. In the end, whether seen through a utopian or dystopian lens, one thing is certain: the political ferment of the past will forever inform the contours of our future.

To truly comprehend our present, we must first understand the waves of change that have crashed upon our nation's shores. May the insights captured herein serve as a guide for the discerning, as America continues to grapple with the ever-unfolding narrative of its own identity.

Appendix A:
Key Figures in the Tea Party and Trump Era

Throughout the whirlwind that characterized the Tea Party and Trump era, several individuals emerged as influential figures. These icons not only shaped the dialogue within the Republican Party but also left an undeniable impact on American political culture as a whole. The following list elucidates key figures who were instrumental in the Tea Party movement and later, in varying capacities, during the Trump administration.

The Tea Party Luminaries

- **Michele Bachmann**: As a Congresswoman, Bachmann's fiery rhetoric and staunch conservatism propelled her to the forefront of the Tea Party movement. She founded the House Tea Party Caucus and was a key voice during its zenith.

- **Jim DeMint**: The former Senator was lauded for his efforts to bring Tea Party candidates into the political arena, significantly affecting the GOP's trajectory through his leadership at The Heritage Foundation.

- **Sarah Palin**: The 2008 Vice Presidential candidate swiftly became a Tea Party favorite, using her charisma to champion conservative causes and endorse like-minded political aspirants.

- **Rand Paul**: Paul's promotion of libertarian principles and his criticism of government overreach resonated deeply within the Tea Party and continue to influence conversations around civil liberties and limited government.

- **Ted Cruz**: As a fresh senator, Cruz leveraged the energy of the Tea Party to become a force within Congress, challenging the status quo and advocating for conservative policies.

The Trump Vanguard

- **Donald Trump**: The embodiment of the anti-establishment sentiment initially harnessed by the Tea Party, Trump's ascension to the presidency marked the pivot of populist ideals from the fringes to the executive branch.

- **Mike Pence**: As vice president, Pence merged his conservative roots with Trump's populist approaches, representing a link between the establishment and insurgent wings of the GOP.

- **Stephen Bannon**: As Trump's chief strategist, Bannon was influential in shaping the "America First" ideology and has been seen by many as a nexus between right-wing populism and the Tea Party ethos.

- **Jeff Sessions**: His early endorsement of Trump and his tenure as Attorney General reflected a hardline approach to immigration and law enforcement that echoed much of the Tea Party's rhetoric.

- **Kellyanne Conway**: As a senior counselor to the president, Conway was a formidable presence and key communicator of Trump's policy priorities and political messaging.

Bridge Figures

Some figures played dual roles, acting as conduits between the transitory period of Tea Party advocacy and the era of Trump's presidency. Their political journeys reflect the evolution of conservative thought during this transformative period.

- **Paul Ryan**: As Speaker of the House, Ryan initially emerged from the ranks of fiscal conservatives akin to the Tea Party and later navigated the choppy waters of the Trump administration's legislative agenda.

- **Marco Rubio**: Rubio's political vision and campaigns reflected a blend of Tea Party enthusiasm for outsider status along with an eventual navigation towards Trump's compelling influence over the GOP.

The individuals listed above were just a fraction of those who steered the prevailing conservative narrative through the tempests of the Tea Party and into the harbor of Trump's Washington. They not only set the political stage but also fostered a movement that would reconfigure the Republican Party's identity and America's political landscape.

Appendix B:
Major Protests and Political Events

In the tracing of the Tea Party's lineage to the Trump era, one cannot overlook the dramatic scenes painted on the canvas of American streets. These protests and political events—collective outpourings of conviction and sometimes, confrontation—shaped the contours of contemporary American politics. They stand as waypoints in our understanding of how fervor in the public square seeps into the halls of power.

The Tea Party itself was born amid a clatter of protests. The Tax Day protests of April 15, 2009, were a cacophony of disenchantment with a government perceived as overreaching in its economic intervention. The imagery was vivid: patriots' garb, Gadsden flags emblazoned with 'Don't Tread on Me,' and placards that demanded fiscal discipline. They signaled a sharp departure from political apathy and ignited a nationwide movement.

Over time, this grassroots activism evolved. The Town Hall meetings of 2009 became battlegrounds of discourse, where lawmakers faced the fiery oratory from constituents. By the time the 2010 midterm elections unfolded, the Tea Party had established a firm foothold in Washington, bringing with it new faces and a new political fervor that was impossible to ignore.

However, the landscape of dissidence wasn't to remain static. The Occupy Wall Street movement of 2011 sprang forth with an alternative view, its tentacles reaching far beyond Zuccotti Park in New York City. They held a mirror to the nation, questioning economic inequality and the consolidating power of financial institutions.

As the Obama years unfolded, issues around healthcare reform generated immense political fracturing and led to significant demonstrations both in support and opposition—culminating in the government shutdown of 2013. 'Obamacare' became a flashpoint, marrying policy debate with public outcry.

The latter years of the Obama presidency were also marked by a series of Black Lives Matter protests. The movement became a prominent feature of the national dialogue on race and justice following the deaths of Trayvon Martin, Michael Brown, and many others. The voices raised on city streets echoed through the chambers of local and federal government alike.

By the time Donald Trump announced his candidacy in 2015, the American political scenery was already deeply etched with the marks of public protest. His campaign and subsequent presidency would see both fierce support rallies and contentious opposition—culminating in the Women's March, the day after his inauguration in 2017. This historic global event was considered one of the largest single-day protests in U.S. history.

Subsequent events, like the March for Our Lives advocating for gun control, and widespread protests over immigration policy, highlighted a social fabric ever willing to express its varied hues. The Trump presidency faced a crescendo of protest in the form of the 2020 Black Lives Matter demonstrations, a nationwide response to the killing of George Floyd.

The tale of American politics across this era is incomplete without acknowledging the January 6th insurrection at the U.S. Capitol in 2021. This event will be long scrutinized as both a result of political movements' invective and a catalyst for further reevaluation of political engagement's boundaries.

These major protests and political events punctured the day-to-day life with a stark reminder that democracy remains a living, breathing, and occasionally tumultuous organism. Their recurrence throughout the past decades underscore this fact: political dynamics can never be detached from the vibrant, vehement voices of the electorate.

The events listed here are but a fraction of the rallying cries that rang out across the nation, cries that coalesced into the forward march of a society grappling with the ideals of governance and the realities of human desire and aspiration.

Chapter 13:
Acknowledgments

As our journey through the complex tapestry of modern American politics comes to an end, it is vital to pause and extend gratitude to those who have made this exploration possible. The pathway from the Tea Party's origins to the Trump era is intricate and is built upon the contributions of many who have offered insights, guidance, and tireless support.

I would like to begin by expressing my utmost appreciation to the scholars and experts whose work laid the foundation for my understanding of the political shifts we've witnessed. Their rigorous analysis and passionate discourse have illuminated the connections that so many have struggled to articulate.

The researchers who contributed to the accumulation of data, the scrutinizing of events, and the tireless sifting through endless hours of footage and articles deserve commendation. Your diligence and commitment have not gone unnoticed, and this work stands as a testament to your labor.

To the spirited activists from all political backgrounds, your fervor and dedication to your causes provided the real-world context that is so often missing from purely academic analyses. The candid interviews and personal stories have been invaluable, allowing me to present a narrative that is both informed and deeply human.

Acknowledgement is also due to my editorial team, whose keen eyes and sharp minds have refined and clarified my thoughts. Your suggestions and critiques have not only improved this manuscript but also challenged me to sharpen my own arguments and assumptions.

I am indebted to the political operatives, both from the Tea Party movement and the Trump campaign, who, often at a great personal and professional cost, offered insights into the inner workings of their respective political phenomena. Your perspectives have been integral to weaving the threads of this narrative.

The historians and political theorists whose coffees I've shared and whose brains I've picked provided a broader context for the current political climate. Our debates and discussions have been both invigorating and enlightening, shaping the critical approach taken in this book.

My gratitude extends to my family and friends for their patience and understanding. The numerous missed dinners and late nights spent typing away at this manuscript were borne of your encouragement and belief in the importance of this work.

The libraries, archives, and institutions that have preserved the documents and material that form the backbone of historical inquiry deserve recognition for their role in maintaining the public record. Without these resources, the research necessary to trace the lineage from the Tea Party to the Trump era could not have been accomplished.

A special note of thanks goes to the various political organizations that allowed me access to their meetings and events. The firsthand experience of your rallies, forums, and debates provided a glimpse into the political process that was both raw and revealing.

My colleagues in the field of political commentary have been a source of camaraderie and competition. Your work has spurred me on to greater efforts, and for that, I am grateful. The conversations and exchange of ideas we have shared form the vibrant ecosystem of political discourse.

To the educators who instilled in me the value of critical thought and the importance of questioning conventional wisdom, I owe a debt of gratitude. Your lessons have resonated throughout this project and in every facet of my life.

The unwavering support of my agents and publishing team has been a beacon during the more challenging periods of writing this book. Your encouragement and belief in the importance of this study have been essential to its completion.

Last but certainly not least, I must thank the citizens and voters whose actions and decisions are at the very heart of the political movements discussed. It is your engagement with the political process that shapes the nation, and your voices that have forged the epoch we now inhabit.

In conclusion, while this book is the product of one author, it stands on the shoulders of many. To all who have walked with me on this journey, discussed ideas, provided feedback, or even simply offered words of encouragement, you have my deepest gratitude. Thank you for helping to bring this story to light.

Chapter 14:
Notes

Throughout the turbulence and triumphs of the Tea Party movement and its evolution into the Trump era, there has been an underlying current of note-worthy observations and lesser-known facts that merit attention. These subtle yet significant points offer deeper insights into the political metamorphosis that has defined the past decade, reflections that are as crucial as they are intriguing.

One could argue that the Tea Party's capacity for dramatic grassroots mobilization found a distinct echo in Donald Trump's ascendancy. The magnate's rallies harnessed a similar energy—a spectrum of passion that drove the Tea Party's rise and, in time, fueled Trump's campaign. The understated symphony of this political vigor remains a testament to the power of mobilized citizenry in the American democratic process.

The sentiments that animated the Tea Party's vigorous protests, such as the disdain for establishment politics and the demand for a return to constitutional principles, did not dissipate into the ether. Instead, these core values were refashioned, taking on a new visage under Trump's banner, lending him a gravitas among voters who yearned for a revolutionary zeal in governance.

The pervasive influence of social media cannot be understated in this political saga. The role that platforms like Twitter, Facebook, and even emerging forums played in amplifying the messages of both the Tea Party and Donald Trump's campaign signifies a revolutionary shift in how political dialogue and mobilization occurs in the modern era.

Financial backing, often a point of contention and curiosity, is another aspect deserving closer examination. While the Tea Party was initially characterized as a grassroots insurgency, the pipeline of support from wealthy donors and organizations suggests a complexity that blurs the lines between bottom-up rebellions and top-down engineering. Trump, too, with his claims of self-funding, painted a narrative that merits scrutiny and reflection.

One must consider the impact of media—both mainstream and alternative—on the perceptions and life span of the Tea Party movement. Similarly, this remains a potent area of exploration in Trump's rise to power. The symbiotic, if occasionally tumultuous, relationship between media entities and these political phenomena are a crucial component of the story.

The judicial system, another cornerstone of the conservative platform, played a critical role in the events discussed in previous chapters. From the Tea Party's crusade against the Affordable Care Act to Trump's consequential Supreme Court appointments, the judiciary remains a battlefield for ideological supremacy.

Examining the Tea Party's approach to policy-making and how it contrasts with that of the Trump administration reveals a tapestry of ideological alignment and divergence. The oscillation between shared goals and distinct methodologies mirrors the broader current of the Republican Party's navigating through populist and traditional conservative waters.

Furthermore, one can't ignore the factor of timing and historical context in this political evolution. The Tea Party emerged during a time of financial crisis and found fertile ground in the discontent of a bruised nation. In a similar vein, the Trump campaign capitalized on social and economic anxieties that had not fully healed, demonstrating the significance of temporal conditions in political escalations.

The fates of specific Tea Party figures, from their ascending influence to their varied paths after the movement's decline, sketch a human element to the political narrative. Their stories provide lessons on the ephemeral nature of power and influence within the caustic world of American politics.

As the political landscape continues to shift, the connections and points of departure between these two factions of the right-wing ecosystem will further influence the ideological undercurrents of the Republican Party. From "Don't Tread on Me" to "Make America Great Again," the evolution of catchphrases signals a transformation in priorities and sentiments.

The Tea Party's initial success in local and state elections is a point that underscores the importance of electoral strategy and the power of momentum. These electoral victories served as springboards, setting the stage for future political showdowns and shaping the battlefield for the Trump ideology to come.

The resistive force the Tea Party mustered against the Obama administration bears similarities to the opposition that met the Trump presidency. This cyclical combativeness within the American polity merits examination, not just for its impact on policy, but for its stress-test on the nation's democratic institutions.

Lastly, there is a subtle thread of American identity that weaves through both movements. The Tea Party's appeals to historical patriotism and Trump's nationalistic fervor reflect an ongoing discourse about what it means to be American in a rapidly changing world.

In conclusion, these notes, while not exhaustive, aim to enrich the understanding of the reader. They bring to light the nuanced choreography of politics, personalities, and power that characterizes the unique dance between the Tea Party and the Trump era. As the

American political stage continues to evolve, these reflections will undoubtedly remain relevant as commentators and citizens alike grapple with the implications of this transformative period.

Chapter 15:
Bibliography

The evolution and the transformative impact of the Tea Party on American politics, and its ideological lineage to the Trump era, is supported by a rich tapestry of sources. Scholarly works, journalistic accounts, and primary sources collectively undergird the analysis presented in the preceding chapters. In constructing the intellectual edifice of this book, a wide array of readings have been meticulously consulted, and it is necessary to acknowledge their contribution to the discourse.

At the inception of the Tea Party movement, it was crucial to delve into its philosophic origins. This research was guided by seminal works such as 'The Whites of Their Eyes: The Tea Party's Revolution and the Battle over American History' by Jill Lepore and 'Boiling Mad: Inside Tea Party America' by Kate Zernike. These texts provided an insightful backdrop for understanding the movement's appeal to the American Revolution and its historical symbols.

The financial crisis of 2007-2008 played a critical role in kindling Tea Party activism. 'The Big Short' by Michael Lewis and 'All the Devils Are Here' by Bethany McLean and Joe Nocera outlined the economic tumult that created fertile ground for political upheaval. The Tea Party's rise was not just a political reaction but a direct response to these underlying economic conditions.

Analyses of political philosophy and core values inherent to the Tea Party were better understood through readings like 'The Constitution of Liberty' by Friedrich Hayek and 'Liberty and Tyranny: A Conservative Manifesto' by Mark R. Levin. The influence of these works indicates the intellectual underpinnings that informed the Tea Party's staunch advocacy for limited government and fiscal conservatism.

Political developments and the Tea Party's ascendancy in the 2010 Congressional Elections are vividly captured in 'The Tea Party and the Remaking of Republican Conservatism' by Theda Skocpol and Vanessa Williamson. This detailed exploration into the movement's integration into the legislative process was paramount to understanding its practical influence on governance.

As fractures within the GOP emerged, we looked to 'Rule and Ruin' by Geoffrey Kabaservice, which details the internal battles and ideological schisms faced by the Republican Party. This book provided context for the eventual rise of insurgent figures within the GOP and the Tea Party's role in cultivating this phenomenon.

To examine the opposition President Obama faced from the Tea Party, works like 'The Obama Hate Machine' by Bill Press and 'The New New Deal' by Michael Grunwald were indispensable. They offered insights into the backlash against the Obama administration's policies and the tactics employed by the Tea Party to mount its resistance.

As the narrative transitioned to the emergence of Donald Trump, it was pivotal to understand his brand of populism. 'The Populist Explosion' by John B. Judis and 'Great Again: How to Fix Our Crippled America' by Donald Trump himself provided foundational perspectives, while 'Unbelievable: My Front-Row Seat to the Craziest Campaign in American History' by Katy Tur offered on-the-ground reporting from the 2016 presidential campaign trail.

To trace the continuities and divergences between the Tea Party and Trump's policies, sources such as 'Devil's Bargain' by Joshua Green and 'Fear: Trump in the White House' by Bob Woodward were of high value. They allowed us to dissect the political maneuvers and understand the administration's internal dynamics.

Stepping back and evaluating the bigger picture, 'How Democracies Die' by Steven Levitsky and Daniel Ziblatt, and 'Identity Crisis: The 2016 Presidential Campaign and the Battle for the Meaning of America' by John Sides, Michael Tesler, and Lynn Vavreck provided the wider democratic context and societal undercurrents within which the Tea Party and Trump phenomena occurred.

Looking ahead, 'The Corrosion of Conservatism: Why I Left the Right' by Max Boot and 'The Road to Somewhere: The Populist Revolt and the Future of Politics' by David Goodhart aided in postulating the future of the GOP and the potential for ideological shifts or continuity post-Trump.

To ensure accuracy and depth, primary sources and documents were also consulted thoroughly. Speeches, policies, legislative texts, and official statements from key figures have been examined to augment the narrative with authenticity and direct evidence of the political zeitgeist.

Let it be noted that this bibliography is not exhaustive of the wealth of materials studied. Nonetheless, it provides a snapshot of the keystone works that shaped the investigation of the intertwined saga of the Tea Party and the Trump era. Every effort has been made to include a cross-section of opinions and analyses, offering a holistic view of the complex political landscape examined within this book.

These sources do more than just inform they ignite the imagination, challenge preconceptions, and provoke thought. For those readers seeking to traverse the same intellectual journey, to explore the currents and undercurrents that sway the ship of state, these works serve as the nautical charts for a deep dive into the turbulent waters of American political life.

Through this bibliography, the reader can appreciate not only the depth and diversity of the research undertaken but also the varying perspectives that stitch together the grand tapestry of ideas that define the political dialogue. The nexus of the Tea Party and the rise of Donald Trump has been a phenomenon that demands rigorous examination and sober reflection, a task to which this selection of sources has been instrumental.